MARLENE DIETRICH'S
A B C

MARLENE DIETRICH
who is to appear on the stage
in an adaptation of the Jacques
Deval play, "Samarkand,"

event, so
sters have
ligibl

MARLENE DIETRICH'S
A B C

REVISED EDITION

An Andrew Velez *Book*

Frederick Ungar Publishing Co.
36 Cooper Square, New York, N.Y. 10003

Library of Congress Cataloging in Publication Data

Dietrich, Marlene, 1904–
    Marlene Dietrich's ABC.

    1. Dietrich, Marlene, 1904–   . I. Title.
II. Title: Marlene Dietrich's A B C.   III. Title: ABC.
IV. Title: A B C.
PN2658.D5A3   1984   791.43′028′0924   84-19573
ISBN 0-8044-6117-1 (pbk.)

MARLENE DIETRICH'S
A B C

Marleine Dietrich claims that beauty is just an illusion. She has maintained the illusion with great success for nearly thirty years, outwitting time and most of her contemporaries.

PREFACE

I am writing this introduction to tell you about the reasons for this new edition.

The main reason, naturally, is "Demand and Supply," the *motto* that guided my professional life, both on the screen and on the stage.

To this I might add my favorite saying:
"The Possible we do immediately—
The Impossible may take a little longer".

My basic opinions remain the same; therefore there are no changes in this book—but some additions to the text and photographs the original edition did not have.

The many letters from most countries of our world asking for the ABC book prompted me to write this new version of my beliefs and my emotional experiences.

MARLENE DIETRICH

A
BSENCE

"Makes the heart grow fonder."

A pretty and poetic thought, but quite misleading. If the person is not around to annoy you, the heart might feel fonder for a short time, but any prolonged absence weakens the bond of love.

The French go a step further: "Absence is to love what the wind is to fire. It blows out the small one and lights the big one."

I cannot argue with this idea too much except to say that there are so few "big ones" that the saying falls into the category of "Wishful Thinking" and there it has its uses.

ACACIA

A beautiful and umbelliferous tree. The perfume one would like to have in a bottle–but all attempts have been unsuccessful.　　　　　　　　　*See* LILAC

1

Sure-fire roles: Top-brass Biblical characters, priests, and victims of the following sad or tragic afflictions:

Drunkenness

Blindness

Deafness $\Big\}$ single or combined

Dumbness

Insanity

Schizophrenia

Mental disturbance

played in successful pictures. The more tragic the affliction, the more certain the Academy Award. The portrayal of these afflicted creatures is considered to be particularly difficult. This is not true. It is more dramatic, therefore more effective.

As the voting for the Award is done exclusively by people belonging to the profession, it is un-understandable that those people should confuse the actor with the task. The public does it constantly, and understandably so. (Some critics do it too, which is unpardonable.)

If the Academy Awards were to be taken seriously, like the New York Drama Critics Circle awards, there would be at least once in a while an award given to an actor who played a mediocre, bad or ineffective part brilliantly in an unsuccessful picture. Another reason for the Academy Award representing a delusion is the fact that the voting co-workers are heavily influenced by either friendship or envy.

A new kind of award has been added—the deathbed award. It is not an award of any kind. Either the receiver has not acted at all, or was not nominated, or did not win the award the last few times around. It is intended to relieve the guilty conscience of the Academy members and save face in front of the public. The Academy has the horrible taste to have a star, choking with emotion, present this deathbed award so that there can be no doubt in anybody's mind why the award is so hurriedly given. Lucky is the actor who is too sick to watch the proceedings on television.

A CAPRICCIO

In the language of music, the designation of freedom in choice.

We should adopt it.

ACCENT

I believe it to be disrespectful to speak another's language with a strong accent. I also believe that an accent-laden speech undermines the authority of the speaker.

There are exceptions, of course. The Latins have a whip hand in this field. Their vowels, their r's, their accentuations are so sweet to *all* ears that they can hypnotize us into believing there is definitely something wrong with one's own correct inflection.

The Latin's only rival is the Russian who uses wrong grammar, wrong pronunciation, wrong inflection with ultimate authority.   *See* LANGUAGES

ACCORDION

A sound I love. Probably because my ear connects it with France.

ACCUSATIVE

The accusative case, frequently (particularly in America)

mistaken for the nominative case, even by well-educated people. Between you and me, it still hurts my ear.

ACHILLES' HEEL

Who hasn't got one! The important thing is to be aware of one's Achilles' Heel and live with it—not fight it.

ACROBAT (*Mental*)

Beware of him. It's interesting but can wear you out, particularly if he is a man and you are a woman.

ACROBAT (*Physical*)

The guy you'd like to be, who makes you feel earthbound, with feet of clay.

ACTOR

An extrovert's profession. A race apart from normal people—those who actor's call "civilians".

AFFECTION

The most necessary food for the soul. More important than humans realize, or want to realize.

See TENDERNESS

AGE

Whatever aging people say to the contrary, we all regret our youth once we have lost it. The famous wisdom that is supposed to be ours in age doesn't help us a bit.

AIMLESS

You can just as well bury yourself if this adjective applies to you.

ALCOOL BLANC

The traditional after-dinner drink of the French. Made exclusively out of fruit. *See* CANARD

ALIMONY

When love is gone it invades the void. *See* DIVORCE

ALLOPATHY

"A system of medical practice that aims to combat disease by use of remedies producing effects different from those produced by the special disease treated."

I'm quoting Webster's only because I have rarely met anybody who knows that the method by which the general public is treated and which is the method practiced by the American Medical Association is called allopathy.

See HOMEOPATHY

ALLOWANCE

In America, all out of proportion, making habitual shoppers out of children and youngsters.

See BOARDING SCHOOLS

ALONE

"He travels fastest who travels alone."

For some people this holds true; for some professions this holds true.

For most of us to be alone is misery.

For women not occupied in a profession that requires solitude, to be alone is absolutely unnatural. A lot of effort and energy is being wasted because women often seem to feel they should conquer the dislike of being alone. That is also unnatural. I readily admit that I hate

5

to be alone. Things to be done in the house or for children or for the man of the house can be done happily alone. But once all those chores are done no woman in her right mind would choose to be alone.

ALTENBERG, PETER

Through him I acquired the courage to fight for my convictions.

Before I had read his works I was and felt like a lone sheep in my reactions to emotional matters.

I quote an example: "While choosing a wastepaper basket they came to a parting of the ways. The man said, "How lucky this happened before our marriage.'"

ALWAYS

My favorite song when I first became conscious of American songs while I was still in Europe.

A word used much by the young.

Closely connected with love because of the natural optimism of lovers and wishful thinking.

AMBITION

Americans are ambitious by nature.

AMERICAN SOLDIER

Lonely men fighting on foreign soil.

In the European theatre of war they did not even have an idea to uphold their mortal hearts.

They fought because they had been told to and had their eyes shot out and their brains, their bodies torn, their flesh burnt. They accepted pain and mutilation as if they fought and fell defending their own soil.

That made them the bravest of all.

ANALYSIS

I have always been against it. Not long ago John Crosby wrote this fine sentence: "Mental blocks have rolled away, and with them all discipline."

See PSYCHIATRY; SELF-DISCIPLINE

ANDERSON, MARIAN

A name which is more a symbol to me than a reality: Marian Anderson. A face, a voice, purity and passion, a dedicated human being who seems to have a mission and is aware of it—harmony and a calm determination reaching out to quiet the restless. I do not know Marian Anderson. I do not have to.

ANGLE

If you want to know the power of angles—study photography.

See PHOTOGRAPHY

ANIMALS

Wonderful creatures, as long as they are out in the open.

ANISE

A sweet-sounding word, meaning baby's biscuits and sweet-smelling wood.

ANTENNAE

Our instincts' cat's whiskers.

See MARRIED LOVE

ANTICIPATION

The wider the scope of knowledge and imagination, the greater the anticipation of tragic events. This is the way of prophecy.

APPIAN WAY (*The ancient Roman military road from Rome to Capua to Brindisi*)

> As beautiful and imposing as you are told it is. You walk on it with awe and feel you are intruding.

APPLE

> A youthful, gay fruit. Meaning red cheeks, children, laughter, good teeth, well-being. "An apple a day keeps the doctor away" is not to be taken literally, but sad people don't eat apples and people who don't feel well don't eat apples. Old people don't eat apples either.
>
> Apples also mean autumn and the countryside. Cool fruitlofts full of green apples. One has to have experienced opening the door to such a fruitloft to know what autumn perfume is. Apples also mean apple trees—in bloom, or heavy for harvest. Peace on earth. "I would like to lie under apple trees and be a soldier no more."*
>
> *Freely adapted from Shi-King.
>
> *See* FARM; AMERICAN SOLDIER

"APRES MOI LE DÉLUGE"

> An expression of Louis the Fifteenth that makes you feel quite courageous and certainly better behaved than saying, "To hell with it."

APRICOT

> The jam of which I like most.
>
> Apricot jam for doughnut filling is best made of dried apricots, first soaked awhile, then boiled slowly in water with sugar and a slit vanilla bean until apricots are mushy. Pass through a sieve—and I mean sieve. Do not

mash them to a pulp in a blender. Passed through a sieve with a wooden spoon, the jam has just the right consistency for the filling. Don't put it on ice.

APRIL

I used to like the word, but since
  "April in Paris,
  Whom can I run to
  What have you done to
    my heart"
rendered with quivering lips and voices full of self-pity, I have lost my liking for April.

APRON

I love aprons. The large white ones with the broad bands and large square pockets. Before "The Lighthouse for the Blind" had them for sale, I used to buy nurses' aprons the old-fashioned kind with all-around gathers. Pockets in a clinging apron don't mean much.

A woman in an apron invites hugging. The apron of a woman flung over a kitchen chair is a wonderful still life. And the pockets of that apron, harboring sticky unwrapped candies, crumpled bits of paper, newspaper ads hastily torn out, pennies and nickels and a ribbon stuck to a band-aid, a baby's sock and a bottle cap, should be food for poets who are so easily tempted to linger on the treasures in a little boy's pants pocket.

AQUA

The first Latin word one learns and remembers. I think that is because it sounds clear and pure and liquid.

AQUARIUS

The great men belonging to this sign have often been misunderstood.

ARCH

A structure of great beauty.

The "Arch of Triumph" (even before it became a vaster symbol during the occupation of France) makes my stomach turn with excitement and love and tenderness and desire. Desire to embrace it, own it, belong to it, etc., etc.

On special days of the year the flag is rigged straight inside the Arch. The position of the Arch is so calculated that although it stands in the middle of Paris there is nothing but sky to be seen through the open space. At night giant arc lights shoot through the space from the ground, streaking the flag with light and continuing into the sky. If you are lucky enough to see this on a windy night, you will carry the image in your mind's eye forever.

ARDENNES (*Woods in southern Belgium*)

One of my not fond memories.

I acquired my worst war wounds there. I froze my hands and feet during the winter of 1944.

ARGENTINA

I like the country. And Buenos Aires in particular. It reminded me of Paris in its generosity of space and the cultivated people I met there. Wonderful, enthusiastic audiences, too, warm and loud. I found the critics astonishingly well-informed about every phase of the

10

theatre and theatrical entertaining. They also understood films and their production, even down to technicalities. I was particularly delighted to be interviewed by ace theatre critics, who, in America, do not usually honor performers like me in that manner.

ARID

Somebody might be interested to know that this word signifies not only "dryness," but also "barren," "unfertile," "lifeless," "uninteresting" and "dull." Or did he know it when he added the second "r"?

ARIES

Aries women like to change positions of furniture ad infinitum. So, if you are married to an Aries woman, forgive her.

ARLEN, HAROLD

You try it. You can't find a bar reminiscent of anything you've heard before. He doesn't even steal from himself. The rich don't have to.

ARMY

Plus-factors for draftees and volunteers:
You relinquish responsibilities—which is very reposing.
You relinquish decisions—which is very reposing.
You gain a definite target to gripe at—which is very reposing.
You are being fed—eliminating again your decision, providing another reason for griping.
You are taken away from Mother—which is high time.
You get a uniform—the most attractive attire a man can

wear: it prohibits you from spoiling your appearance should you have bad taste. You relinquish another decision: what tie to choose. Girls trust you.

You learn—discipline, mental and physical.

You learn—to live with other people.

You learn—how to take it.

You learn—*esprit de corps.*

You learn—to pull in your belt.

You learn—to surrender privacy.

You learn—that you can stand much more than you thought.

You learn—to live by a timetable.

You learn—to put up with rude awakenings.

You learn—cleanliness (if your mother never quite succeeded).

You learn—to cook and to peel potatoes and to bear the unavoidable with dignity.   *See* WAR

AROMA

The best I know is captured in an Alsatian wine called *Gewürztraminer*.

ARROGANCE

On some people it looks good.

ARROWROOT

Makes a good starch and babies' biscuits.

ART

A much abused word.

ARTICHOKE

Great remedy for the overworked liver. In liver-conscious countries, you can buy concentrated artichoke juice in pharmacies. In Italy there is even an aperitif made out of artichoke juice. Just try eating a couple of artichokes instead of lunch and dinner and watch your headache disappear. It takes a little longer than drinking the juice, but as long as you can't get any in America it is your logical substitute.

ARTICULATION

Modern actors often substitute nonarticulation for "down to earthiness."

Particularly, the school of acting which I call the "Looking-for-the-other-shoe method" employs nonarticulation to help the "naturalness" along. The L.F.O.S. method gets its name from the attitude of the actor, who, let's say, plays a proposal scene sitting on a bench. He never looks the girl in the eye—turns his head away from her, bends over, looks to all sides and almost under the seat while delivering his lines, hesitantly, as though his entire concentration was being absorbed by the search for the other shoe.

British actors articulate. They learned it when they started out in the theatre and cannot help but articulate. They are not obsessed with "naturalness" at all costs, as many American actors are.

The film actor has an easier time if he chooses not to articulate; the audiences' ability to lip-read during close-ups helps the ear. He also is blessed with a most conscientious watchdog: the sound engineer.

ARTIST

The genuine ones are precious people with an unending stream of stimulation flowing toward you.

Generous people, humble people; often sad, which makes them lovable because their sadness has a valid reason.

ASPIRIN

In Europe, strictly a medicine.

In America, a habit, almost a food. Children swallow it at the slightest provocation, and the habit is instilled in them. When an American child has a headache he gets an aspirin. In Europe, thank heavens, children's headaches are very rare. They are considered a danger sign. If no stomach upsets explain a headache, doctors are consulted, eyes are examined, etc. I believe that aspirin has its medicinal value but should not be dispensed so easily by mothers of today.

ASSISI

A most wondrous village. If you go there, try to arrive at night.

ASTAIRE, FRED

Elegant! Elegant! Elegant!

ASTROLOGY

Lexicographers call it a pseudoscience.

I would like to argue with Webster's about the wording: ". . . the supposed influence of the relative position of the moon, sun and stars on human affairs." It is the phrase "human affairs" I argue with. "Human beings" would be more correct.

Agreed, one can debate the type of influences, but how one can deny the influence is beyond me. The arrogance which causes such denial is gigantic.

The human being is not made of such different matter that it can remain untouched, uninfluenced by those same forces that exercise their power day and night on bodies far stronger than the human being. Nobody argues with the fact that the moon attracts the waters of the earth—the timing of the tides being related to the individual quarters of the moon. Nobody argues either with the farmer and the gardener who know when the moon is "right" to sow or plant. Nobody argues with the effect the full moon has on certain human beings: sleepwalking. Nobody can argue with the fact—not widely known—that the police department increases the staff on nights of the full moon. (Human emotions fly high on those nights. Experience is the best teacher.) In short: What conceit to think that we human beings are immune to influences of which we have acknowledged the power. The fact that we cannot put our mental finger on the exact form these influences take cannot give us the audacity to deny them.   *See* SUNSPOTS

AUSTRIA

A soft country. Blue-caped Madonnas painted on houses. The tempo of life is easy-going—understandably so because of the beauty of the country. Not the grandiose beauty of its neighbor Italy. A cosy, tender beauty—fitting the waltzes, the young wine, the violins, the food.

Nothing is harsh. Not even the German language. The Austrians speak it caressingly, adding vowels at the end of words and using a lot of diminutives. The melody of the language is chanting. The people have much of the French character, and the great thing they have in common with the French is *charm*. We say "they eat charm by the spoonful" once they are born. "Live and let live" is another similarity.

Poets: Altenberg, Schnitzler.

Composers: Johann Strauss, Richard Strauss. (He *could* be Austrian because of *Rosenkavalier*.)

AUTHORITY

Necessary to possess when in a position of leadership, may it be in a home, office, etc., or governing towns, states, and countries.

Requirements for authority: knowledge not only of the general matter, but also of the problems confronting all departments working toward the same end. Nothing undermines authority faster than a gap in the familiarity with every facet of the particular subject at hand. Any man assuming authority in a cooperative undertaking must be able to judge achievements and contributions and retarding elements legitimately interfering with the results. Most people in a position of authority who *are* equipped with knowledge, understanding, tolerance, dedication and love for their fellowmen, are respected and loved.

AUTOGRAPHS

People never ask for autographs for themselves. Autographs are always for nieces, nephews, wives, children, uncles, aunts, or the girl or boy friend. The request for the autograph, most of the time, is made in restaurants, for example when one just puts a piece of meat in one's mouth and is about to swallow it. It is always preceded by the sentence "I hate to disturb you but. . ."

The wrath of those nieces, nephews, etc., is held up as the bugaboo for the urgency and the strange object being extended to you. Those objects are: tiny pieces of paper, the inside of matchbooks, handkerchiefs, dollar bills, ties, paper napkins, and more of such objects that refuse to accept the ball-point ink. The ball-point pen in question is not extended to you. All autograph seekers, with very few exceptions, seem to think that the victim of their pursuit has a pen permanently attached to his hand. Other people are inconvenienced, and waiters usually come to the rescue. While one writes or tries to write, the conversation continues in the same vein: The autograph seekers—by now there are many of them—are trying to destroy any suspicion that the autographs might be for themselves. This must be triggered by a desire not to appear immature.

If I have the chance to see a person that I worship or admire, I do not hesitate in the slightest to ask for his signature, as long as I do not inconvenience or embarrass the object of my admiration. I even frame the signatures of those wonderful people.

AXIS

Among other things, it means: an alignment of countries. Long ago, this word used to be a derogatory word. It meant: the countries aligned against the United States, namely: Germany, Italy, and Japan. Now that we are

17

asked to forget the recent unpleasantness (except on certain official national holidays), our State Department might find the word useful.

who could not only design clothes, but could cut a piece of material on the body and pin and sew a perfect replica of his sketch. I have not known any other Paris designer who knew so much about the actual making of clothes, therefore knowing what was possible and what wasn't, what materials and what cuts were correct for any given design. The more the boss knows, the more the employees have to know. The first fitting at Balenciaga was like the third fitting at any other house.

BASIL

The aroma of all meat is greatly enhanced by a bit of basil. People on salt-restricted diets should use basil in most foods. It's wonderful on buttered spaghetti.

See DILL

BATHS

I love them except they make me lazy.

I don't like them, though, when I am alone in the house. It feels as if the bathtub were a giant, quiet sea—makes you feel quite forlorn.

BEATLES, THE

I loved the Beatles and despised the person who broke them up.

BEAUTY *(The Seamy Side)*

The emphasis on visual beauty, particularly in America, is taking on dangerous proportions. Dangerous especially for the youth. The youth of today are thrown into utter confusion almost systematically, and I consider it a miracle that they manage to survive with some sanity.

One of the doctrines, adding considerably to this confusion, looks harmless at first glance. I believe it to be far from harmless—the Desire to be beautiful. This is a universal instinct, and it is easy to see how this desire, properly goaded, has every chance of getting out of hand. Once out of hand, it becomes the cause of much unhappiness. The young girl of today is the unhappy victim. I wish I could say the innocent victim—she is almost innocent. But let us take her side; she deserves it.

The necessity of possessing beautiful looks is being pounded into the heads of young girls all over the country. Their eyes are drowned in urging ads and slick articles on artificial means for obtaining this all-important "passport to success." Before they have time to think for themselves they are deluged with apparently bonafide endorsements of such power and onslaught that they cannot help but accept as a fact the thesis that if you are beautiful you have the world on a string. And who would not want to have the world on a string? Particularly if you can get hold of that string without any effort. Wanting things the easy way—being lazy—is normal and nothing to be ashamed of. Like wanting to have your cake and eat it too—not a bad idea at all.

The avalanche of promises thunders along. All have the same basic theme: If you are beautiful, you can taste all the delights there are, choose or reject according to your whim and appetite; pursue Beauty, and you pursue Happiness.

That is the *why* of this searching for beauty, this chasing of the golden ball. It promises to roll us easily into the Paradise of Happiness.

The ugly girls do not fare so well. The glass slipper

does not fit. Prince Charming is oblivious to their frantic efforts. The Beauty does not have to try hard. Everything that is good, everything she desires, falls right into her beautiful lap.

In the beginning it seems just like a bed of roses. For her everything is *special*. General rules do not apply. She has an extra-special set of rules all her own. Didn't she always get that extra candy from the grocer ever since she could walk? Didn't Mother always melt and forgive when she begged with those big, big eyes? Didn't Mother always buy that extra bow, that special dress she really didn't need? Didn't Mother make many added efforts to show her off so that she would be chosen to play the angel or the fairy-princess, although she really was much too young?

And later, when her bracelet was full and heavy with charms and the boys were swarming around her, wouldn't her mother cock her proud head to the side and say, "I don't know how she does it, my little Beauty"? It was not her fault that she relied on looks to get her heart's desires, once she saw that it worked.

And the more it works, the more value she puts on this asset, the more effort she puts into its presentation.

This preoccupation with beautiful looks leaves no time to think, and for a while all goes well, the cream of life is hers. She gets away with murder at 150 miles an hour. She has no real joy, but she does not notice that. She has little infatuations and calls them love. She hasn't time or resources to think and feel a multitude of things. She circles around uncomfortable tasks as a cat circles around hot milk. She spends her time doing nothing; she is busy, but she does nothing. The time is spent on a vague kind of living, being bored most of the time with frequent interruptions of aimless shopping, cocktails, sitting in beauty parlours, gabbing on telephones, playing cards or almost reading a newspaper. She neither knows nor cares what goes on in the world so long as it does not directly interfere with her schedule. Does the discontent she's bound to feel make her look for the reason in herself, or does she blame the world, and buy a hat for consolation?

This state of heart is the main cause of the restlessness. It is the reason why such girls seek emotional stimulus in variation. It is the reason why, when the fun begins to fade and nothing is there to replace it, they take their hearts from bar to bar for that one more drink which might bring satisfaction—a fruitless, endless search.

They didn't have to be bad to end up in discontent. But, being beautiful, they needed extra portions of integrity and self-discipline just to stay afloat.

Most beautiful women are not natural champions in self-analysis. Recognizing inner faults is an uncomfortable business. Eliminating inner faults is an even harder task. Disguising them is not easy; and even if one succeeds temporarily, one is left with a feeling of guilt. Guilt again is uncomfortable, so it is convenient all the way around not to prod too deeply into the inner self.

Except for the poor women on psychiatrists' couches you will never hear a woman say: "I am bad" or "I am wicked." You might hear "I was bad," meaning: "I did something bad" or "When he said *that,* I really was *wicked* for a moment and said. . ." Women profoundly believe that they can be bad or wicked whenever they choose to be, and all the while be little angels at heart. (They are wrong.)

When it comes to outside beauty, it is a different story. In that domain they readily admit their flaws, and the disguise is easier and much more fun. We all have come to accept those disguises without feeling evil. So, we paint our cheeks, mouths, eyes and eyebrows, our own and false lashes, every inch of our face, we powder, underline and outline with black and brown and blue and green and gold and silver, we bleach one day and dye the next, cut and add just as we please, throw specks of silver and gilt on cheeks and hair, and feel not a speck of guilt.

All that pursuit, and still there is no happiness in sight. In the realm of love and happiness or happiness and love, beauty lies like a feather on the scale of values. This is one of the most shocking realizations that can come to the beautiful girl.

This realization often arrives at a time when it is too late to change the pattern of her thinking, her responses and her evaluations. Therefore, her logical reaction is resentment. From then on she is caught hopelessly in the net of discontent, and no one can help a discontented woman. *See* UGLY DUCKLING

BECAUD, GILBERT

He wrote the most beautiful love song ever written. I sing it in three languages.

All over the world there is rarely a dry eye in the theatres.

His talent as a composer overshadows his talent as a performer.

25

BED

"It's a good thing or it's bad, but beautiful!" (Lyric by *Johnny Burke*)

BEEF TEA

Liquid steaks. Ideal food for the convalescent, children lacking appetite, weak and old people.

4 pounds round steak cut in cubes put into a mason jar. Heat the closed jar in a pot of water slowly boiling for 4 hours. The liquid that you will find in the jar is enough food for a daily ration of a grown-up. You can add salt and pepper for the healthy, dilute it with water for children, adding vegetable salt. Use while fresh.

BELLE-MERE

The French chose this word to give to the mother-in-law. It means: beautiful mother.

I wish all nations would adopt it.

And it would be nice if comedians could get along without their tired, tasteless jokes about mothers-in-law.

It would be especially nice for mothers-in-law.

See MOTHER-IN-LAW

BELMONDO, JEAN-PAUL

New blood, new looks, new vitality, new *fluidum*, new eroticism, new normality for that malady-ridden strain of today's neurotic actors.

BERGMAN, INGMAR

They treat him like a king and when you are with his disciples you fall right into step.

He lives up to his title when you meet him.

His humour matches his imagination.

When he was planning his first film in color he sent his entire staff to have their eyes examined for color blindness.

BERLIN

An island in Germany which produces the Berlin sense of humour: a sharp, dry, matter-of-fact wit mixed with gallows and laugh-at-yourself humour, a tragic humour devoid of reverence or self-pity. The jargon of the Berliners is among the most descriptive and daring in the world.

BEST DRESSED LIST

This list is reserved for the rich, those who can afford to buy from the great designers, who have time for endless fittings and then can be seen wearing these creations in the right surroundings.

BIRCH TREES

They touch my heart.

BISMARCK

He was first to express the belief that it is in the best interests of the victor to restore what he has destroyed.

BISTRO

When you are really hungry,
When you don't want to dress up,
When you want to feel at home,
Go there.

BIZBUZ

A Hebrew word meaning "waste," which I have added to my vocabulary because it sounds more humorous and not as accusing as "waste." *See* WASTE

BLOOD

If the blood flow to any part of the body is restricted, trouble follows. It is on this knowledge that the science of osteopathy is founded.

BLOOMINGDALE'S *(New York Department Store)*

My Mecca. The harbour of supplies for demands SOS'd to me by family, friends, acquaintances—usually ten minutes before closing time.

BOARDING SCHOOLS

What a blessing they are. Particularly for boys. The harassed fathers of today should try to manage at least some years of boarding school for their boys. Mothers and fathers of today cannot give their children the quiet, unnervous, unchanging atmosphere and treatment they should receive. Teachers and educators are trained not to have their troubles colour their behavior toward children. I believe that the unevenness of parental reactions toward their children is responsible for much of the "emotional insecurity" of our young generation. British and Swiss boarding schools are my favorites.

BOATS

I am happy on a boat, even if it goes nowhere and is tied to the dock. Boats give me a feeling of peace and quietness.

BODY

A heavy body weighs down the spirit.

BOOKS

You do not love a book necessarily because it teaches you something. You love it because you find affirmation of your thoughts or sanctions of your deeds.

BOOTH, SHIRLEY

She came onstage. Said: "Hello." And had me crying.

BORDEL

A country without bordels is like a house without bathrooms.

BOSOM

Today's fad requires large, soft, hanging breasts that can be easily displaced.

Beautiful breasts cannot be pushed together, cannot be pushed out. There is stubbornness in their firmness.

See BRASSIERE

BRADDOCK, MRS. BESSIE, *M.P.*

Inborn tact, gentleness in a rough shell.

BRASSIERE

In America something strange has happened. A man will turn his head, or whistle, if that is his fashion, on seeing an obvious contraption, a clearly outlined steel construction under a dress or, even worse, a sweater.

This is rather touching and only proves what an idealist man is.

BROADWAY

A shuffling parade. Faces hungry for everything but food.

BUBBLE

Music to Mother's ears.

BURTON, RICHARD

I truly loved his Welsh soul and admired him as a man
and as an actor. In my book his only fault lay in his
unhappy choice of women.

I also admired him for his capacity to hold his liquor.

BUTTERMILK SOUP

Buttermilk to which you add, chopped: boiled ham,
cooked shrimp, fresh cucumber, hard-boiled egg, lots
of dill, salt, pepper. Put on ice. Serve with ice cubes
floating in it. You are the boss, you know how much
of each item you like in this wonderful Russian soup for
summer evenings.

JOSEPH VON STERNBERG
THE BLUE ANGEL (1930)
The appearance of neo-romanticism.

Ihren größten Triumph feierte Marlene Dietrich in dem deutschen Film „Der blaue Engel". Fast über Nacht stieg sie durch ihre Darstellung der Lola zum Weltstar auf. Holiywood wurde aufmerksam und holte die Berlinerin hinüber.

ALVADOS

The elixir we drank mornings to wake us up for action.

See ARDENNES

CAMERA

A friend of mine.

We understood each other.

CANADA

What a beautiful country. The air and the sky seem to have been freshly washed and polished, and the people too. Like the Swedes, the Canadians have un-northern temperaments. Such capacity for enthusiasm!

CANARD

Dunking of a cube of sugar in alcohol or coffee—permissible in France. Also permissible: to make noises while sucking the liquid out of the cube and to dunk again to

31

refill. It is not permissible at official dinners, but there you rarely feel in the mood for a *canard* anyway.

See ALCOOL BLANC

CANDLES

In churches and when electricity fails they are all right.

CAPA, BOB

In the Ardennes I traded my fur-lined cap for something utterly useless he offered in return. He was solemn that icy night. There were icicles in his hair.

It was the last time I saw him before he was killed.

CAPRICORN

Anyone with troubles can unload them safely onto Capricorn's shoulders.

CAR

A car is a man's best toy.

CAR SICKNESS

If you have children prone to car sickness, carry quartered lemons with you. Give them a piece to suck on. It does wonders.

CAUSE AND EFFECT

A logical event that no wishful thinking can erase.

CAVALIER

A species that is dying out.

There is a difference between the cavalier and the

gentleman: A cavalier can never forget his manners; a gentleman can.

CAVIAR D'AUBERGINE

Bake an eggplant in oven till the skin is black. Let cool. Chop half of a medium-sized onion very fine. Fry it golden brown in 4 tablespoons of oil. Peel eggplant and cut in small pieces. Add to the onions and fry for a couple of minutes while mixing constantly with a wooden spoon. Add one small can of tomato sauce (Spanish Style) and keep on mixing. Transfer to chopping board and chop very fine. Serve cold as an appetizer.

CEZANNE, PAUL

His watercolours are among my greatest joys.

As a man he had many admirable qualities, but the one that appeals to me most was his distrust of fame, a quality he shared with Rilke.

See RILKE, RAINER MARIA

CHAMPAGNE

As a symbol it has extraordinary powers. It gives you a Sunday feeling, and better days seem just around the corner. If you can manage to have ice-cold *Dom Pérignon* in a beautiful glass on the terrace of a Paris restaurant looking onto trees in a midday autumn sun you will feel like the most luxurious grown-up in the world, even if you are used to drinking champagne.

CHAMPIGNONS *(Mushrooms)*

Cook 2 pounds of mushrooms in water not quite covering

them, with salt, a few peppercorns, a small onion and a bunch of fresh dill which is tied together after you cut off the coarse stems. (It is easier to fish out the dill later when you tie it with a thread.) Mushrooms give a lot of water so be sure not to drown them at the start. (The broth has a wonderful taste when it is not too thinned down.) Once they are cooked you can chop them or mash them in a blender. Add a piece of butter, a bit of white wine, and serve as a "mousse" with steaks or veal scallopini. Or you can make a very wonderful soup.

Soup: Melt 2 tablespoons of butter, add 2 tablespoons of flour, stir till smooth. Slowly add mushroom broth, little by little, constantly stirring, only adding more when butter and flour thicken again each time you have added the broth. Stop adding liquid when the consistency is that of a thin soup. When you add the mashed mushrooms, they further augment the thickness. Add dry white wine to taste. Chop dill very fine and sprinkle before serving. Put sour cream on the table; some people love to put a teaspoonful into their soup.

CHARLATAN

The name given by medical men to any medical man who uses means to treat illnesses not yet used by the medical men and judged by them according to standards sanctioned by the A.S.A. *See* QUACK

CHEAP

Nothing that is cheap looks expensive.

See EXPENSIVE

CHEAP SKATE

In America: what the name implies.

In Europe: a great delicacy served with capers and black-brown butter.

CHEVALIER, MAURICE

The master of the most difficult and hazardous branch of the theatrical profession.

CHEWING GUM

A pacifier for adults.

CHILD

"I do not love him because he is good, but because he is my little child." *Rabindranath Tagore*

CHILDREN OF ISRAEL

Like the cows in India, they are holy, *and* they know it. It shows in their faces, and their eyes are clearer than other children's eyes.

CHINCHILLA

The most unbecoming of furs. Only made desirable because of the complete absence of weight.

CHOCOLATE

Chocolate and brandy
Chocalate and calvados
Chocolate and whiskey
Chocolate and anything resembling alcohol
All make a good soldier's breakfast.

CHRISTMAS

Quiet festive days uniting families, not loud gatherings devoted to drink. *See* NEW YEAR'S EVE

CHURCH BELLS

Many too few of them in the United States.

CIGARETTES

I started smoking during the war. I have kept it up ever since. It keeps me healthy.

CIRCUMSTANCES

The correct use of this word is with "in" not "under."

CIRCUS

The fascination that the circus and circus life holds for us all—at a certain time of our life—stems from the elementary wanderlust, the elementary rebellion against an orderly bourgeois existence.

CITIES

Any special love for a city is invariably connected with emotions that have nothing directly to do with the city.

CLOONEY, ROSEMARY

She is bathed in sunshine, tenderness, clarity of spirit.

COCTEAU, JEAN

He had the wonderful habit of suddenly writing a letter to tell his thoughts regardless of long silences from the other end.

With a generous hand he picked up the thread as if it had never slackened.

COFFEE

It is a splendid drink and all that,
And the national drink of America,
And how about a nice cup of tea?   *See* TEA

COLETTE, SIDONIE

She was a Catholic. She had been divorced. The Church refused burial to Colette.

The ingenuity of the French found a way to pay homage to their respected idol. A ceremony was held in the courtyard of the Palais-Royal in Paris.

It was a cold, bright, quiet autumn day. The coffin stood high on a pedestal; the French flag loosely draped over it.

At the sounding of the fanfares a slow wind began to play with the flag. The eulogies spoken by great writers and statesmen echoed from the patina-buildings.

The wind circled the coffin, lifting the flag and settling it gently back onto the black wood. Soon the words of the speakers were no more than an accompaniment to the game the wind was playing.

It crept under the flag and billowed it, undulated it—as a child plays in the evening under the sheets.

The ceremony ended and the mourners left, trying not to let their steps resound on the stones. The wind did not leave.

It continued the game with the flag in the vast, empty courtyard.

It might well have been a message from the Keeper of the Gate.

COLOURS

The joy they give us dwindles with the years.

COMPASSION

Without it you mean little.

COMPLEXES

I am getting tired of people alibiing for their bad manners by citing their complexes.

COMPLICATED PROCEDURES

Man hates them. When every accomplishment of his woman takes on the importance of a small miracle, he'd rather do without the miracle.

See DRESSING *(To go out with your man)*

COMPOSERS

My favorites: Ravel, Franck, Debussy, Richard Strauss, Stravinsky.

CON AMORE

With love.

Used as direction in music: Tenderly.

See TENDERNESS

CONSCIENCE (professional)

My professional conscience has enervated quite a lot of people except, naturally, my teacher, guru: Burt Bacharach, who loved it.   *See* BACHARACH

CONTENTMENT

The Cinderella of emotions.

COOKBOOKS

Judging by the vast amount of cookbooks printed and sold in the United States one would think the American woman a fanatical cook. She isn't.

COOKING, 1

It is natural that a woman should cook. Her inborn mother instinct wants to feed. Her real motherhood makes it imperative that she should cook.

It is easy to cook simple things. Children like simple things. Men like simple things. They don't crave variety in their pleasures as much as one might think, once one has found what they like. If one cooks, one knows two joys: to watch people one loves eat, and to watch people one loves eat what one has cooked. Cooking does more than just give joy. It occupies one's hands constructively. One of the greatest occupational therapies there is.

See HOUSEWORK

COOKING, 2

The secret and the challenge of cooking is anticipation.

COOKING WITH GAS

is "Cooking with Gas."

Every recipe I give is closely related to cooking wth gas. If forced, I can cook on an electric stove, but it is not a happy union. I cannot vouch for the result. I have cooked in hotel cupboards on an electric plate and have managed to feed eight Frenchmen on *pot-au-feu*, but that falls into the category of outstanding achievement beyond the call of duty. If you attempt to cook well and not be a nervous wreck when you sit down with your guests or your family, cook on a gas stove. You have *control* over gas heat. You can have a hot flame at a moment's notice and bring it down to medium or low or very low or put it out at a moment's notice. Without this you have to traffic your pots and pans as if it were rush hour on your town's busiest corner. You stall before the plate gets hot if you need great heat immediately, and once you have achieved that and want less heat you have to pull your pot or pan away from the red-hot glowing circle until it has cooled sufficiently to push pot or pan back onto it. You have to stay there and direct traffic. A gas stove liberates you from such occupation. You turn the high flame low and are free to do other chores necessary to get a dinner on the table. Don't get too frustrated reading my recipes if you love your electric stove. You are stuck with it.

COOKING *(What to do when. . .)*

When you have added too much salt to soups, stews, etc.: Add a large peeled potato and cook it for at least 20 minutes.

When your pots have black spotty watermarks: Boil water with potato peels and vinegar.

When the whites of eggs don't beat stiff enough: Add a tiny bit of salt.

When you used yolks and don't know what to do with the whites: Add a few drops of lemon, a bit of toilet water and you have a very good hand lotion.

When boiling or stewing meat does not want to get tender: Add a tiny bit of bicarbonate of soda—or vinegar.

When your cake won't come out of the mold: Leave it face down and wrap a wet towel around the mold. The cake will slide out in no time.

When you can't trust your stove and the crust of your cake gets too hard: Put a tin bowl filled with water into the oven while you bake.

When you don't want to watch the clock and want your boiled eggs soft: Put them to cook in cold water; when the water boils, they are done.

When everything sticks to the bottom of your frying pan: Rub it with a piece of lard; don't use it for a couple of days but nourish it with lard while you let it rest.

See FRYING PAN

CORNED BEEF

A most persistent childhood memory is that of feasting on corned beef sent to us by our fathers serving at the front. American soldiers would throw the cans over to the enemy when the war of trenches quieted down by nightfall and the crickets made peaceful sounds—which is how my father described it in his letter.

COURAGE

"Courage is the fleeing forward." *E.M. Remarque*
"A peculiar kind of fear they call courage."

Charles Rann Kennedy

I think that in war, innocence fathers courage at the start. Later it is sheer optimism.

COWARD, NOEL

His surname belied him. He was as brave as a lion.

CREDIT SYSTEM

The American Tragedy.

CROQUE-MONSIEUR

Emergency lunch or dinner.

Into a flat baking pan you put slices of rye bread cut in halves onto which you have put two thin slices of boiled ham and topped it with a thin slice of Swiss cheese. Fry for two minutes on the open flame and bake in medium oven till the cheese has melted just a bit. The bread will be crunchy, the ham juicy, the warm cheese will look like Swiss cheese, not like a sauce.

CUCUMBER SALAD

Peel cucumbers not from the narrow end down. The narrow end is often bitter and your knife transfers the bitterness to the entire cucumber. Cut off both ends. Slice very fine into a bowl. Add salt. Mix. Put a smaller bowl inside the bowl containing the cucumber slices. Press down. Put into the refrigerator for at least half an hour. Longer if you have time. When you are ready to serve, squeeze the juice which has gathered in the bowl out of the cucumber slices with your hands. Utensils or machines won't do. Proceed with your favorite dressing. Oil and vinegar and dill, or sour cream and dill go best with cucumbers. *See* SCHNITZEL

CYNICISM

It is so foreign to me that I am paralyzed with astonishment when I meet it.

CYPRESS

The symbol of mourning.
It is a true symbol.
Cypress trees lining a road: a sight of sad beauty.

D
ALI, SALVADOR

A great painter.

Don't let the shiny side fool you.

DANCE

The men I like to talk to are invariably nondancers.

DANISH KISSEL

You cannot make the heavenly Russian dessert *Kissel* without the Russian berry.

Here is a substitute.

Make the American sweet called "Danish Dessert."

But instead of the indicated amount of water use the juice of canned sour cherries.

Mix defrozen raspberries with it, boil till transparent.

Cool. Serve with sour cream.

DAUGHTER

Your daughter is your child for life. *See* SON

DEBROUILLER

Se débrouiller is a special talent the French have and which they consider a frequent, necessary occupation.

It means to manage to get out of tight spots, difficulties and uncomfortable situations.

Someone particularly apt is called a *débrouillard.* Finding things that are difficult to find also falls into the category of a *débrouillard.* Children complaining they have forgotten their homework assignment are told:

"Debrouille-toi!" which can mean anything from "Go and see one of your classmates and find out" to "Find a good excuse to tell the teacher." To be able *se débrouiller* belongs to the practical education of the French.

Whenever France is in trouble we say like a prayer: *"Elle se débrouillera."*

DEMAND AND SUPPLY

My Credo. Give what is needed. "Let them eat cake" is too easy. By the same token: If nothing is needed, give nothing.

DE SICA, VITTORIO

His film *Miracle in Milan* contains this scene: Destitute people scrambling out of railroad shanties, unwrapping newspapers from their shivering bodies as they hasten toward a circle of warmth. There they stand motionless, huddled together in a shaft of sudden sunshine.

DIAPER SERVICE

Any mother who knows what it means to wash and boil diapers will gladly renounce pleasures, even food, to be able to pay for the diaper service.

DIARY

Diaries of famous writers surely have been written with some part of the brain contemplating publication.

DIETRICH

In the German language: the name for a key that opens all locks. Not a magic key. A very real object, necessitating great skill in the making.

DILL

The best herb I know. Obligatory for: fish, shellfish, mushrooms, cucumbers, sour cream, buttermilk soup, lettuce, dill sauce. If you like dill as much as I do, try it on fried potatoes. It doesn't sound right, but it is.

DIMINISHED RESPONSIBILITY

In my lifetime I could never have gotten away with "Diminished Responsibility."

Nowadays you can get away with *murder*–literally.

DISHWASHING

A woman can stand at the sink, damp under the spray of her dishwashing, the steam in her hair. She, like Phoenix out of the ashes, can emerge and be utterly desirable afterward. She has magic powers. The man has not. Anyway, not when he is being domesticated. A man at the sink, a woman's apron tied high around his waist, is the most miserable sight on earth. No woman should make her man wash dishes.

She did not find him at a kitchen sink when he first caught her fancy—or, if she did, he was the plumber.

DISREGARD

With a good deal of disregard for oneself, life is a good deal easier borne.

DIVORCE

Theoretically I am against it.

Practically it is quite another story.

Avoiding divorce at all cost can bring misery and tragedy to both parties as well as to their children. "Let's stay together for the children's sake" is a fine theory. If one can manage a harmonious home for the sake of that theory—all well and good. But how few humans can?

DO IT YOURSELF

A great antifrustration medicine.

Think of the millions of people on assembly lines occupied in making, fitting, screwing, welding, gluing, filing, adding parts and *only* parts onto, into *other* parts, never seeing the finished object, not even seeing in their mind's eye the ultimate combination of those parts.

The male mind cannot take this thwarting lightly.

So, when a man, doomed to such piecework throughout the week, can, with the help of a "do-it-yourself" kit, make a little footstool in his backyard or garage on Sunday, the satisfaction of the accomplishment is comparable to the emotion Leonardo da Vinci must have had when he looked first upon Milan's cathedral, or when the opening of the locks began and the waters gushed successfully along the Martesan Canal.

Children are rather bored with the "do-it-yourself" craze, for the simple reason that they have been at it since time immemorial. *See* SELF SERVICE

DOSTOEVSKI

My enthusiasm for him burned high through my teenage years, and to this day I know passages of his stories by heart. "White Nights" and "The Tender One" used to make me quite drunk.

DRESS *(On a budget)*

Here are some basic rules: Don't ever follow the latest trend, because in a short time you will look ridiculous. Don't buy green, red or any other flamboyant-colour dress. A small wardrobe must consist of outfits that you can wear again and again. Therefore, black, navy blue, and grey are your colours. Don't buy separates. Don't believe the sales talk that you can have five dresses for the price of one. And don't buy cheap materials, no matter how attractive the dress looks to you. Don't say you can't afford a dress made of expensive materials. Save up for it. If you have one good suit, preferably grey (navy gets shiny), two black dresses, a black wool skirt, a couple of black and grey sweaters, you'll be well dressed most of the year until summer, when you'll wear simple cotton dresses. Another suggestion, don't send your clothes to the cleaner's all the time. Spot-clean and press them yourself. It's worth it because they last longer. And while you're saving for that good black dress, on your next date wear a black sweater and skirt. Nothing

wrong with that as long as you don't ruin the elegance
of the outfit by overemphasis of the bosom.

See BRASSIERE

DRESSING *(To go out with your man)*

When you have a dinner date, be prepared so that you
can dress without delay. Be ready on time. Even if you
should appear a dream personified, and he has waited
hours to take the dream to dinner, you've spoiled the
evening. His over-hungry stomach won't let his eyes see
all your beauty, his mood is bad, and by the time he's
had his coffee and his mood is fine, you are quite angry
and not beautiful. *See* ORGANIZATION

DUTY

"Duty means loving that which one makes imperative
upon oneself." *Goethe*

"But what is your duty? The demand of every day." *Goethe*

Marlene Dietrich appearing with The Beatles — George, Ringo, Paul and John.

EARNING

There is a gigantic difference between earning a great deal of money and being rich. *See* RICH

EATING

All real men love to eat. Any man who picks at his food, breaking off little pieces with his fork, pushing one aside, picking up another, pushing bits around the plate, etc., usually has something wrong with him. And I don't mean with his stomach.

EDUCATION

Education has become the fashion in America. Education has always been better in the countries of our friends abroad. It took the realization that the standard of education is higher in a country that we regard with some fear, to make us seriously consider meeting that standard. It is a sad reason, but better than none.

EGGS

Scrambled: To each batch of three room-temperature eggs, add one extra yolk, salt; beat with a fork, not wth an egg beater. Heat butter to golden yellow, not brown. Pour the beaten eggs into it, flame low, turn slowly with the fork. Turn out flame. Keep turning with the fork to desired consistency. Serve immediately.

EGOCENTRIC

If he is a creative artist, forgive him.

EINSTEIN, ALBERT

His theory of relativity, as worded by him for laymen: "When does Zurich stop at this train?"

ELECTRICIANS

The electricians who populate film studios are all out of the same mold, a mold which, happily, has not been thrown away. They are the backbone of the studio. Great individualists, craftsmen with an extra eye for detecting phoniness. They are not impressed by fame, only by excellence. This holds true for every nationality. One can work in a film studio anywhere and be home.

See PROPERTY MAN

ELEGANCE

Rarely found today. Women are not brought up to know about it and therefore lack even the desire to acquire it.

See FASHION

EMBARRASS

To embarrass anyone falls into the category of bad manners. In America it is practiced almost like a sport.

51

EMERSON, RALPH W.

"Do not say things. What you are stands over you the while, and thunders so that I cannot hear what you say to the contrary."

I have gooseflesh when I read this, think of this, or write this down.

ENGLISH

A beautiful language and a rich language, yet most of us neglect the beauty and use only a fraction of the riches. Even worse, we pedal through life on our small vocabulary, detouring thought in roundabout words.

See WASTE

ENVY

I do not know envy. I do not know how this happened. I can only guess that I was taught to enjoy things regardless of ownership.

EREMIOPHOBIA

Many Americans are afflicted with eremiophobia. They are the best customers of radio programs, the best customers of companies manufacturing recordings of sounds and music which help them combat the stillness they fear.

The record companies outdo radio by flooding the market with records eliminating decision on the part of the listener. The titles of those records give a clear picture of the nature of the phobia. There is:

Music to Change Your Mind By
Music to Nip By
Music for a Bang

Music for Cards
      for Conversation
      for Cuddling
Music for Peace
      for Meditation
Music for Expectant Mothers
Music to Make Housework Easier
There is even: Music for Trapping.
But to me: Music to Read By is the cat's meow.

See KOAXOPHILIA

ERMINE

In white it is quite out of fashion today. Dyed black it is a very elegant fur, best used for jackets to wear in the afternoon and evening. It is much less expensive than it looks.

ESTIMATED TAX

The enforcement of this law is the United States Government's most un-American activity.

This law demands payment of taxes on salaries that may eventually be earned by the taxpayer long before he actually earns such salaries. Should the "estimation" prove to be too optimistic, or entirely a mirage, the government will return to the taxpayer the "wrongly estimated" taxes at the end of the year—without interest.

Read it again. Your eyes have not deceived you.

See WITHHOLDING TAX

EXPENSIVE

Expensive things *look* expensive.

There is always a connoisseur in the crowd.

See CHEAP

EXTENSION CORD

Make it your traveling companion.

EXTRAVAGANT

It is a completely subjective evaluation and therefore one should never criticize another person's extravagance.

EYES

I like light eyes. The changes in expression and emotion are beautiful to see.

Marlene Dietrich in "Golden Earrings,"

④ Fix' Pläne, die Weiterreise nach Amerika zu verhindern, scheitern jäh. In Yokohama findet Fogg seinen Diener in einem Zirkus wieder, und sie fahren gemeinsam nach San Franzisko. Dort landen sie in einer Kneipe, in der die Wirtin und ihr Pianist die Gäste bestens unterhalten (Bild Nr. 4). Da hier außer den Sitten auch die Messer locker sind, müssen die beiden Engländer fluchtartig das Feld räumen.

F
AIRBANKS, JR., DOUGLAS

An American who picked up and digested all the good things and *only* the good things during his life outside his native land.

FAIRY DUST

We all like it—whatever the time of our lives.

FAIRY TALE

The certainty of the happy end is the magic of the tale.

See HAPPY ENDINGS

FAME

If fame *would* be synonymous with fortune, wouldn't that be fine?

FARM

I would like to live on a farm. Not a modern farm, mind you, but a simple old-fashioned farm with cows and pigs and goats and chickens and ducks and horses, where every day is the same except for the seasons bringing a different kind of work. I would have a vegetable garden, and from the kitchen I could look over a wheat field. I would work hard all day long and feed a lot of people, preferably more children than grown-ups. I would have a big, square wood-burning stove with low benches on the side where we would sit in winter and warm our backs. And in summer there would be large copper kettles on the stove with fruit and sugar cooking for hours, the preserve jars lined up on the long kitchen table, and in the fall mushrooms on the stove, freshly picked in the woods nearby. There would be a small river to calmly fish in. The farm should not be too far away from a small village, and I would set my clock by the sound of the evening church bells. I would like to sit on a bench in front of the house when the day's work is ended or lie under an apple tree. *See* APPLE

FASHION

Don't follow it blindly into every dark alley. Always remember that you are not a model or a mannequin for which the fashion is created. *See* ELEGANCE

FASTING

You must have an important reason to be able to fast. If you don't, you must make an oath to yourself, an oath important enough to take the place of the important reason. Vanity is not enough of a reason. Health isn't

56

either, as long as you feel well. Make a time limit for the fasting. A day, for instance. It is easier to fast one day entirely than to eat a little for a week. It is very healthy to do that. Don't think you are going to collapse on the street. Drink water and go to bed early.

FATHERS

Most fathers struggle to give their sons chances they themselves never had. But, recognizing the deficiencies of their own education, how can such fathers escape the dilemma of making untrained judgments concerning the education of their sons. A king, realizing his incompetence, can either delegate or abdicate his duties. A father can do neither.

If only sons could see the paradox, they would understand the dilemma.

FATIGUE

"The sad fatigue of idleness." *Matthew Green*

See IDLENESS

FEAR

A fatal surrender.

FEET

The poor things! What we do to them once we are away from Mother's watchful eye.

Most men take their shoes off whenever they can.

Most women take their shoes off whenever they can.

And don't men wish they could do it as inconspicuously as women!

FEMININITY

Woman's greatest asset. Her own magnetic field into which the man is drawn.   *See* LOVE and MARRIAGE

FENNEL

Weak fennel tea: the best medicine against baby's colics.

FILM CUTTER

He puts the pieces together.

Nothing fazes him. He cannot only change the action, but, by clipping tiny frames of film to speed it up or by adding tiny pieces to delay it, he can also change reaction.

He can cut sound with the skill of a surgeon and can, if need be, cut out a breath and draw no blood.

See SOUND MEN

FISH

I like boiled fish. Most people would, but they don't because experience has taught them differently. Almost any fish tastes wonderful when properly boiled. There is no secret or skill to learn.

Take the fish out of the refrigerator a good half hour before you cook it. Boil water with salt, peppercorns, one large onion cut in half, large bunch of dill, bunch of parsley for half an hour. Take out the green bunches. Put in your fish, or the filets, or the slices of fish. Cover. Put out the flame. The fish must only steep, it must never boil. When your slices are very thick it takes longer. When the slices are thin or when you cook filets of sole it takes not more than three minutes of steeping.

You must have everything ready and on the dinner table when you put the fish into the boiling water. You cannot wait for people to sit down once you have put the fish in. You cannot let the fish wait either, steeping in the water. You have to take it out the second there is no raw part to be seen when you break a bit in the middle with a fork. If you leave it in the water after that you'll be sorry, so take your time and serve an appetizer first so that you have your customers cornered.

Drawn butter to which you add a few drops of lemon and a lot of chopped dill, and new potatoes cooked in the skin, peeled, and tossed in drawn butter, then salted, are the best additions. Also lettuce or romaine with lemon and oil, salt and pepper and parsley. Don't serve a salad with a strong dressing.

FISHING

I love it—the calm of fishing in a small, lazy river lined with trees and meadows. For bait I use a sandwich of worms and tomato. I can swear to it that fish love red.

See FARM

FLAG

It takes great strength of character never to lower one's flag. Exemption: taxi drivers.

FLEMING, SIR ALEXANDER

My admiration and devotion are indescribable. Even if I would tell all about my experiences during the war years, I could not describe the godlike image Sir Alexander Fleming became and remained for me.

FLEXIBILITY

A great asset for body and mind.

In advanced age both tend to rigidity.

One of the reasons why young people find it difficult to live in close contact with the old is the loss of the mind's flexibility.

Rigidity of thought, decision, opinion is by no means reserved for the old, but the danger of becoming rigid of mind increases with the years.

Old people are most conscious of their stiffening bodies; they are completely unconscious of their stiffening minds.

FORGIVENESS

Once a woman has forgiven her man, she must not reheat his sins for breakfast.

FRAISES DES BOIS

The tiny wild strawberries of France. Only when you have tasted them do you know what summer tastes like.

FRAME

If something written or drawn on paper is precious to you, frame it. You won't lose it. People have a curious respect for anything that is framed.

FRANCE

I learned the language when I was four years old. I loved the country long before I saw it and the people long before I met them. I am very happy with that love which bears no trace of logic or sanity.

FREEDOM
The execution of self-imposed duties proves freedom.

FREE-LANCE PHOTOGRAPHERS
My pet hate.

FRIEDMAN, TUVIAH
Let's remember him not because he caught a rat, but because he made it possible to try the rat; not for the sake of punishing the rat, but for the sake of millions of minds that had grown careless about remembering wrongs and millions of minds who might overlook the extent of the wrongs in history class.

FROSTING
For doughnuts. Put confectionery sugar into a bowl, add lemon juice and rum, a very little at a time to taste till the consistency is like a thick soup. Mix and stir well with wooden spoon.

FRUSTRATION
Frustration can exist only if one sets one's cap for something out of reach. It is self-inflicted, and the moaning which goes on about this fashionable affliction bears no resemblance to logic.

FRY, CHRISTOPHER
He even looks like a poet.

FRYING PAN
The queen of your kitchen. Be gentle with her. Don't

scrub her inside with steel wool or detergents. Right after using, wipe her clean of grease with soft paper towels, then rinse immediately with hot water and dry with paper towels. She will be smooth; she will not cling to the things you don't want her to cling to. But you cling to her as a good subject should.

FUNCTION

One must function at all times *and* according to requirements.

FUNERAL

The accusing finger of your own conscience spelling out "nevermore."   *See* SERMON *(Funeral)*

Arriving at a full cinema for a performance of *Black Fox*, Dietrich seats herself on the floor of the stalls next to property millionaire Felix Fenston and his wife, formerly Greta Borg. In the film Dietrich narrates the story of the rise of Hitler

THE CADS: West Berlin officials today ungallantly revealed the age of Marlene Dietrich. They said she is 62. Her birth certificate, lost in the battle of Berlin, was found in an East Berlin registry office. *4-6-64*

G ABIN, JEAN

A magnificent actor without knowing the tools of the trade. Rough outside—tender inside. Easy to love!

GALLOWS HUMOR

Adopted from the German: *Galgenhumor*. Meaning: The ability to laugh at one's own fate when directly confronted with disaster.

It might seem strange that such a word should originate with the Germans, who, as a nation, are not blessed with a sense of humour.

My gallows humour was Hemingway's great joy. It was one of the reasons why he made me his friend.

See BERLIN

GARDEN

"Let us take care of our happiness, go into the garden and work." *See* HAMMOCK

63

GARDNER, ERLE STANLEY

During the war his books were the saviours of minds encased in freshly torn bodies.

GARLAND, JUDY

A victim of injustice.

I transferred my love for her to her daughter Liza.

See JUSTICE

GEMINI

I like the *joie de vivre,* the vitality, the speed, the absence of chichi in Gemini women. My women friends happen all to be born under that sign.   *See* ASTROLOGY

GENDER

At the best of times gender is difficult to determine.

In language gender is particularly confusing.

Why, please, should a table be male in German, female in French, and castrated in English?

French children, for instance, are male even if they are girls, in English there seems to be considerable doubt, in German they are definitely neuter.

Even more startling is the fact that the French give the feminine gender to the components of the male anatomy that make him male, and the male gender to the components of the female anatomy that make her a female.

In view of all this let's keep a stiff upper lip.

GENERAL DE GAULLE

The personification of my beliefs and code of conduct.

When he made the unique speech in June 1940, he put me in his pocket for life.

Whatever he did or said afterwards I do not try to evaluate. He could do no wrong.

GENEROSITY

A great luxury reserved for the rich who rarely take the opportunity to enjoy it. Most people with truly generous tendencies don't have the means to be generous with.

I am not talking about the generosity of tax deductible donations. I am talking about the generosity neither talked nor written about.

GENTLEMAN

A man who buys two of the same morning paper from the doorman of his favorite nightclub when he leaves with his girl.

GERMAN MEASLES

The German measles are called *Roeteln* in German. But the English-speaking countries have another children's sickness called roseola, which is also *Roeteln* in German.

Something has been added there and although I have done a lot of research I have made no headway.

GERMANY

The tears I have cried over Germany have dried.

I have washed my face. *See* ISRAEL

GIACOMETTI

I fell in love with the dog he sculpted and decided to

tell him so when I came to Paris. There was a heated sympathy between us from the start. I carried a fragile statue in my arms across the Atlantic. He brought it to me, wrapped in newspaper, just before I left.

GIRDLE

An unattractive object. Women have immense faith in the miracles a girdle can produce. I believe they are laboring under a false illusion. I don't feel equipped to argue too vehemently about the pros and cons of girdles, except to say that the natural line of a woman's body has its points.

GLAMOUR

The which I would like to know the meaning of.

GLASS SLIPPER

Most women are addicted to shoes in all shapes and forms.

The manufacturers are well aware of that fact.

They also know that a woman will abandon a pair of shoes easier than a dress, which can be altered according to changing styles. So they change the styles as much as the narrow limits allow.

They dagger-point the toes, they square them, they stub them, open them, close them. They point the heels, spike them, widen them, square them, elongate them, lilliput them, open them, close them, ad infinitum.

Faced by this *embarras de richesses* women seem to have become slightly mixed up and don't know anymore what every woman should know.

Here are some simple pointers:

Don't wear super-high spike heels with suits or street dresses. Don't wear open-toe shoes with suits, or when you want to be elegant in the afternoon. I know they are comfortable, but *elegant* they are *not*. Wear them with summer dresses when the sun shines; don't wear open toes in white, black or brown or navy blue, *ever*. Wear them only in colours not contrasting with your stockings. If the colours are close your toes won't stick out like sore thumbs. You are just as well off without white shoes altogether: White shoes make your feet look large and fat.

Patent-leather shoes might make you feel nice and daring. *Elegant* they are *not*. The same goes for bright red shoes. (You *can* wear them with a summer dress though.)

Whether your budget is small or medium, your best buy for summer and evening shoes is blonde or beige. You can wear them with every dress, even with black, so long as they are a continuation of your stocking colour. Your legs look longer when the colour of your shoes doesn't act like a stop sign.

Do not wear slippers on the street. I mean the high-heeled shoes that have no straps at all. Shy away from plastic shoes with handbags to match. Shy away from bows, flowers, clips, tassels and such.

If you want bells on your toes, tinkle them at home.

GLOVES

Gloves belong to suits, afternoon and evening dresses. Outside stitching on gloves is strictly reserved for sport suits and dresses.

Don't waste money on black gloves. They clean very badly and make you sad.

One good rule to obey: Do not put your gloves back on when leaving a party or a restaurant. Once they are off, they stay off.

GOETHE

My idol. From him came all the answers to all questions in my *Sturm und Drang* years.

His was the courage of extremes. He sanctioned love without condition, without pride.

I was not only taught but embraced the rules he set: "To be doing the right thing, whether what is right eventually comes to pass being of no concern—to abhor ignorance in action—to regard perfection as the norm of heaven."

GOOSEBAY

That air one should bottle.

GOSSIP

Nobody will tell you gossip if you don't listen.

GOULASH

Make it at least four hours before dinnertime so it can steep standing covered near the heat after it is done. You need a pot with a thick bottom or a Dutch oven. 2 pounds of goulash meat (backside, beef or veal) cut in squares. One pound of onions chopped very fine. Fry the onions golden brown in butter, add paprika, stir. Add the meat, but see to it that all the pieces touch the bottom of the pan. Salt, coarse pepper (more paprika for

MD

M.D. and Josef von Sternberg (<u>see von Sternberg</u>)

The Blue Angel (1930)

L

Morocco (1930); (<u>see Tilly, <u>Vesta</u></u>)   L

Morocco (1930);
M.D. and Gary Cooper

Morocco (1930);
M.D. and Adolphe Menjou

L

L

Shanghai Express (1932);
M.D. and Clive Brook
(see Femininity)

L

Shanghai Express (1932); (see <u>Women</u>)

Blonde Venus (1932)

L

The Scarlett Empress (1934)   MD

L

The Devil is a Woman (1935)

M.D., 1936, (see Fashion)

MD

M.D. and Mae West (see West)

MD

Manpower (1941): (see Camera)

MD

M.D. and Noel Coward
(see Coward)

MD

M.D. with GIs (see American Soldier)

AV

M.D. and Erich Maria Remarque (<u>see Remarque</u>)

MD

MD

M.D. and Jean Gabin (<u>see Gabin</u>)

M.D. and Burt Bacharach
(<u>see Bacharach</u>)

MD

MD   *Witness for the Prosecution* (1958);
on the set with (<u>from left to right</u>) Charles Laughton,
M.D., Tyrone Power, Billy Wilder (director)
(<u>see Laughton</u>)

*Around the World
in 80 Days* (1956) left to
right: Cantiflas, David
Niven, M.D., Frank
Sinatra (<u>see Sinatra</u>)

AV

M.D. and Mike Todd
(see Todd)

MD

MD

M.D. and Judy Garland (see Garland)

Touch of Evil (1958, directed by Orson Welles)
([see Welles](#))

AV

M.D. and Charlton Heston
on set of *Touch of Evil*

AV

MD   M.D.

M.D. and
The Beatles
(see Beatles)

MD

M.D. and Gilbert Becaud (see Becaud)

MD

M.D. in tails (<u>see Tilly, Vesta</u>)

M.D. with Jean Cocteau and
Jean Pierre Aumont (far right)

MD

MD

M.D. (<u>see Glamour</u>)

the veal). Let fry while turning so that onions do not get burnt. Should your meat give out enough liquid to start stewing instead of frying, cover your pot. If it has not done that, but the meat is frying and has browned nicely, add broth or water to barely cover it. Cover pot. When liquid is gone and a brown crust starts to form on the sides and bottom, shake a bit of flour through a tiny seive over the meat and stir for a few seconds. Then add enough broth or water to cover the meat. Low flame. Simmer till tender. To the veal you add the finely scraped peel of half a lemon and a chopped tomato after you mixed the meat with the onions. When you use beef you can add garlic to the onions in the beginning and a teaspoon of white vinegar after you've added your liquid.

Before serving, you can add sour cream if you like, or just put it on the table. Some people prefer goulash without sour cream. Do not put the goulash into the refrigerator after it is done. It won't spoil. Nothing will happen to it. Leave it near the heat of the stove until dinnertime. It gets better the longer the meat is allowed to soak in the sauce; next day it is even better.

If you can find a German butcher you will be safer as far as the choice of the meat is concerned. American butchers in their endeavor to give you "the best," might give you meat that is too lean and therefore gets dry during long simmering. The meat from the middle back and shoulder is gristly and has fat running through it. That is what you want.   *See* SCHMALZ

GRANDMOTHER

Judging by the world press, I am the only grandmother

in the world. Should there be any other grandmothers around, I salute them all.

Ours is a great joy and a great task.

Here are the rules:

1) We must tiptoe at all times.

2) Never tiptoe on anybody's toes.

3) Be there when needed.

4) Never be more than "Mother's helper."

5) Disappear when not needed.

6) Bear without self-pity the sudden silence in our own house.

7) Keep both ears cocked at all times for that call to action.

8) Be ready when it comes.

See MOTHER-IN-LAW

GRAVE

O love, while still 'tis yours to love!
O love, while love you still may keep!
The hour will come, the hour will come,
    When you shall stand by graves and weep!

Ferdinand Freiligrath

My mother quoted this poem incessantly.

The same thing said by George W. Childs: "Do not keep the alabaster boxes of your love and tenderness sealed up until your friends are dead."

GREENLAND

Should be called Iceland. The trickster who tried to lure settlers there must have had his hand in misnaming another island. *See* ICELAND

GRIEF

Grief is a private affair.

GRUMBLING

Grumbling is the death of love.

HABIT
Often mistaken for love.   *See* MARRIED LOVE

HAMBURGER
Easy to make, easy to eat, easy to decide upon, easy to get, and Hamburg had nothing to do with it.

HAMMOCK
The ultimate of quietude.
The *Do Not Disturb* sign in a garden.

HAMSUN, KNUT
My first self-discovered literary love. I loved the simplicity, the absence of adjectives, the poetic repetition. I really did.

HANDBAG

The man who pronounced all women's handbags a luxury-tax item must have been out of his mind. In the next life he might be born an alligator and die truly as a luxury handbag. Or he might be a woman enchanted to haunt department stores and supermarkets crowded as at Christmastime, children in tow, tot in her arms, clutching money, keys, shopping lists, identification card, handkerchief, gloves of her brood and her own in her one unoccupied hand. That will teach him.

HANDS

I like intelligent hands and working hands, regardless of their shape in relation to beauty. Idle hands, stupid hands can be pretty, but there is not beauty in them. Of course, children's hands are miracles from every point of view.

HAPPINESS

I do not think that we have a "right" to happiness. If happiness happens, say thanks.

HAPPY ENDINGS

I love happy endings. I do.

HARDWARE STORE

I'd rather go to a hardware store than to the opera. And I like the opera. The hardware store's only rival is the stationery store. When you arrive in a strange town and the unfamiliarity makes you uncomfortable, like dampness creeping into your bones, the hardware store is Disneyland, Treasure Island, King Solomon's Mines.

See STATIONERY STORE

HARMONY

I need harmony around me more than food, drink, and sleep.　　　　　　　　　　　　　　　*See* PEACE

HATE

I have known hate from 1933 till 1945. I still have traces of it and I do not waste much energy to erase them. It is hard to live with hate. But if the occasion demands it, one has to harden oneself deliberately.

I do not think I could hate anyone who does harm to me personally. Something greater than myself has to be involved to cause me to hate.

See AMERICAN SOLDIER

HATS

They can be great fun. And it is *true* that they can put a woman in a good mood. Anyone who laughs at this fact just knows nothing about the finer points of woman's capacity for survival.

HAUPTMANN, GERHART

As he had been a Nobel Prize winner, we studied his works in school. Although I had great respect for my literature teacher, I revolted at her respect for Hauptmann's plays.

She wrote a spanking note in red ink at the bottom

of my essay on his works. I remember her mentioning the enthusiastic acknowledgment he had received in the United States.

When I met learned men in America, I inquired about Hauptmann. I found out that they had changed their minds and admitted to having overrated him. This pleased me no end, particularly because Hauptmann had just become an important member of the Nazi Party.

HEALTH

"The preservation of health is a duty. Few seem conscious that there is such a thing as physical morality."

Herbert Spencer

I cheered when I found this.

HEALTH FOOD

It doesn't only sound good, it tastes good, feels good and does good. But it is difficult for the working person to eat only "Health Food." If one cannot eat "Health Food" all the time, one should eat it like a cure each year when on vacation. This is better than nothing.

HEAVEN AND EARTH

A great meal for summer evenings, a peasant favorite because it is good and cheap: apples (for heaven) and potatoes (for earth). Cook tart, sliced apples with sugar or, better, honey, or make applesauce. Boil potatoes, peeled or with the skin. Put two bowls on the table. Everyone has his own way of mixing the fruits of heaven and earth.

HECKART, EILEEN

If she were acting in Europe, she would be Queen of the Boards. In America, the typecasting barbarism deprives the world of her true talents.

HEIFETZ, JASCHA

The sound of his strings, so perfect, so pure, that sometimes I wish he would descend from his height and be human.

HEINE, HEINRICH

His poems: romantic, longing, with more than a tinge of irony.

His life: voluntary exile in France, the right components for the pedestal he stands on.

HEMINGWAY

My personal Rock of Gibralter. Even now. His letters are locked in my heart and under lock and key in a safety deposit box.

HIGH-FASHION

The extreme one rarely sees except in magazines devoted to the cause.

HIPPOCRATIC OATH

Just read it and realize that BY OATH doctors must cover up for each other's mistakes.

See MEDICAL ETHICS

HIROSHIMA

The bomb that fell on Hiroshima fell on America too.

It fell on no city, no munition plants, no docks.

It erased no church, vaporized no public buildings, re-
duced no man to his atomic elements.

But it fell, it fell.

It burst. It shook the land.

God, have mercy on our children.

God, have mercy on America.

Hermann Hagedorn, 1946

These lines appear in the 12th edition (1948) of
Bartlett's Familiar Quotations. Is it a sign of our times
that they have been left out of the 13th edition (1955)?

HITCHCOCK, ALFRED

When he directed it seemed as if he didn't. But he did,
he did, and how he did!

HOLLAND

Everything cozy.

HOLLYWOOD

When I came to Hollywood, the great era of silent films
was over and done with. The village was not "gay and
reckless" anymore. The studios operated like any other
establishment—one had to clock in at a certain hour and
heaven help you if you failed to do so. It remained like
this all through the rest of the thirties until I left to join
the army.

Today, when so few films are being made, Hollywood harbors more television actors than film actors. "Hollywood" is dead.

HOMEOPATHY

"A system of medical practice that treats a disease by the administration of minute doses of a remedy that would in healthy persons produce symptoms of the disease treated."

There is much more to this important system than Webster's definition.   *See* ALLOPATHY

HONESTY

"It is so convenient to be frank and honest."   *Nietzsche*
He meant "toward other people," naturally.   *See* TACT

HOPE

"Hope, the dream of the waking man." (Ascribed to *Aristotle*)   *See* OPTIMISM

HOROSCOPE

Skeptics, bear with me. Have your child's horoscope made. There is no other way to know his character traits and his emotional makeup before he is old enough to express them himself. The knowledge you gain from the horoscope will help you to know where to exert your influence and where to relax. You will have an indication of his weaknesses and his natural strengths; in other words, you will not waste efforts and wear him out if you know that his nature will guide him on its own power. On the other hand, you will be wise to the characteristics that need your guidance. If you have many children, the horoscopes will be your answer to many riddles. Although you may have brought up all your children in the same way and even in the same home and neighborhood, you look at them sometimes wondering how on earth they could be so different in character and reactions. You will have found out that you have to handle each one differently, but have had to learn it the hard way, alone. If you have their horoscopes, you have the beginnings of explanation long before the time.

See ASTROLOGY

HORSES

The sound of horses' hoofs on pavement gives me nostalgia.

HOUSEHOLD VIRUS

The household virus is not known to the medical profession in general. It is well known, though, to pediatricians. When junior has eaten too much chocolate cake or devoured too much ice cream or frozen his stomach with iced drinks hastily poured down on a hot summer day, when drafts catch baby in the crib or when the night cools off suddenly and makes an icebox out of the nursery before Mother knows it—the virus takes the blame.

Since the harm is already done, why should the pediatrician blame Mother and give her a guilty conscience? It's much better all around to blame that "virus" that is "going around." Daddy, who has faithfully remained old-fashioned as far as his children are concerned, is forced to unwrinkle his brow when he asks for the cause of the "sick leave." The household virus has been at it again—and nobody feels guilty.

See PEDIATRICIAN

HOUSEWORK

The best occupational therapy there is. It is also the most useful occupational therapy. It is one of the rare occupations that show immediate results, which is very satisfying, to say the least.

HUMANITY

"What humanity needs is not the promise of scientific immortality, but compassionate pity in this life and infinite mercy on the Day of Judgement." *Joseph Conrad*

See QUOTATIONS

Once in a generation... a motion picture explodes into greatness!

Spencer Tracy Burt Lancaster Richard Widmark
Marlene Dietrich Judy Garland Maximilian Schell
AS IRENE HOFFMAN
AND Montgomery Clift

STANLEY KRAMER'S
Judgment at Nuremberg

Ingrid's New Film

Roberto Rossellini was preparing to start a new movie, *Europe 1951*, in France on Feb. 1. The film's star: Rossellini's wife, Ingrid Bergman. It will be her first film in two years.

Movie of the Week

The Blue Angel, 20-year-old German film which first brought Marlene Dietrich fame, was revived with English subtitles. The story, about a professor (Emil Jannings) who falls in love with a singing hussy, still has impact. So does the younger Dietrich (*r.*).

Marlene Dietrich 20 years ago.

I CELAND

Should be called Greenland.   *See* GREENLAND

ICE WATER

A curious American beverage.

IDEALS

We need ideals, not competition, to be a well-functioning nation.

IDLENESS

It is a sin to do nothing. There is always something useful to be done. I have no respect for those idle rich who discharge their duty to be useful by staging charity balls.   *See* USEFULNESS

IGNORANCE

Forgivable, except in a responsible job willingly undertaken. *See* GOETHE

IMAGINATION

"Imagination, not invention, is the supreme master of art as of life." *Joseph Conrad*   *See* QUOTATIONS

INCOME TAX

I should of stood in bed.

INDEPENDENCE

Financial independence is a many-splendored thing. It makes it easy to stick to your codes, your principles, your beliefs, and keeps you from ever having to prostitute yourself.

INDIFFERENCE

"The tragedy of love." *Somerset Maugham*

How do you know that love is gone? If you said you would be there at seven, you get there by nine and he or she has not called the police yet—it's gone.

INFUSION

The nightcap of the French. A delightful institution. Besides warming you in winter and cooling you in summer, it is very good for your system. Some infusions are sheer perfume:

Verveine
Tilleul (Linden)
Menthe (Mint)
Camomille

Fleur d'orange
Passiflore
Serpolet
Guimauve
Queue de Cerise

INSURANCE

Insurance is what you take out to protect your property. But should you, after years of paying your premium, lose your property, the insurance company will grill you like a criminal, label you a bad risk, and cancel your policy. This is their way of punishing you for losing something in the first place.

INTELLIGENCE

Superior intelligence kindles my love.

INTIMACY

There are more imaginary specks of dust casually brushed off gentlemen's shoulders by women wanting to show intimacy in public than there are real specks of dust desirous of settling on gentlemen's shoulders.

INVEST

What you should have done and never did because baby needs shoes.

ISRAEL

There I washed my face in the cool waters of compassion.

ITALIA

Beauty everywhere.   *See* ROME

ITALIAN MEN
Beautiful "hot air."

IVY
Good outside the house, bad inside.

See SUPERSTITION

VEDETTES A T

Dans son der** film, la plus jeune des grand-mères et l'a** des jeunes premières un peu mûries, Mar** Dietrich, joue les veuves (plus ou moins) j**uses. Le voile donne un charme nouveau à visage qui, si l'on peut dire, a conquis monde grâce à ses jambes.

J

ACKPOT

Milktoast and hothead, genius and simpleton, the scream is assonant when they hit it.   *See* LAS VEGAS

JARGON

Something one should use only after one has learned the legitimate language fully.   *See* LANGUAGES

JASMINE

Plain jasmine, night-blooming jasmine; give me jasmine anytime.

JAUNDICE

The noncontagious kind used to be cured in Europe by Karlsbad salt.

JEALOUSY

An uncontrollable passion, the Siamese twin of love.

JEANS

Sometimes I like entire towns or places just because I don't ever have to get out of my jeans.

JEWS

I will not try to explain the mystic tie, stronger than blood, that binds me to them.

JOB

One of my favorite people in the Bible. Also my favorite book, written by Joseph Roth.

JOIE DE VIVRE

How few of us have it; and what a great gift for the person who has it and the people who witness it.

See GEMINI

JOUVET

An actor after my own heart, a great director. His approach to actors is best described by citing one of the many Jouvet anecdotes:

The Actor: Monsieur Jouvet, what am I supposed to feel when I declare love to the girl in the first scene?

Jouvet: Don't feel, my boy. Play, play.

See STANISLAVSKI

JUSTICE

I am a fanatic on the subject. To be just should be taught to children as soon as they understand a language.

K ANT, IMMANUEL

His laws, my roots.

"Act so that the maxim of your will can be valid at the same time as a principle of universal legislation."

"The direct opposite of the principle of morality consists in the principle of one's own happiness being made the determining principle of the will."

"A man must first appreciate the importance of what we call duty, the authority of moral law, and the immediate worth that obeying it gives a person in his own eyes, before he can feel any satisfaction from consciousness of his conformity to it, or can feel bitter remorse that accompanies consciousness of transgressing it.

"Indeed, it is the duty to establish and cultivate this sentiment that alone properly deserves to be called moral sentiment."

"Moral law, not requiring a justification itself, not

only proves the possibility of freedom, but proves that freedom really belongs to those beings who recognize this law as binding on themselves." *See* LOGIC

KETCHUP

If you have to kill the taste of what you are eating, pour it on there.

KIBBUTZ

Israel's lifeline. The materialization of the errant Jew's dream: owning and cultivating his own land.

All kibbutzim, large or small, are mainly engaged in agricultural work. Each member is solely concerned with the prosperity of his community, his kibbutz. He works eight hours a day, and more when emergencies demand it. His needs are taken care of by the kibbutz. Food, clothes, cigarettes, housing, his children's care and education, medical care and hospitalization, care of his elders, are all the responsibility of the community. Trained nurses take over the newborn babies and bring them up. The mothers work for the kibbutz. They visit their children at the end of the day, but their and their husband's energy and vitality is directed solely toward the growth and flourishing of their community.

The schools go up to the eighth grade. The students also do manual work as part of their education. Everything is issued, clothes are washed, repaired, replaced. There is no money in rotation; there is no need for it.

Many of the young kibbutzim are situated near the border, and the saga of the young ones defending their land in the War of Independence in 1948 added an important chapter to the history of the old-new nation.

The marvel of the now-fertile Negev Desert can be traced directly to their toiling hands and the sweat of their brow.

KIBITZER

An ardent spectator who gets involved in proceedings without taking any responsibility. Oddly enough, his presence is not resented, but often desired. Personally, I like kibitzers—but it depends on where they do their kibitzing.

KIDNEYS

Watch *them* and not the bags under your eyes.

See CAUSE AND EFFECT

KINDNESS

Practice it; it's easy. Just put yourself in the other person's shoes before you talk, act, or judge.

See COMPASSION

KING-SIZE

I'm agin it.

KISSES

Don't waste them. But don't count them.

See WASTE

KITCHEN

I dislike the modern antiseptic small kitchens. The kitchen should be a place where the family can gather and eat while Mother is cooking. I venture to say that there is a parallel between the modern American kitchens and the modern American family problems.

KNIVES

The greatest joy in the kitchen. Keep them sharp.

See HARDWARE STORE

KOAXOPHILIA

In *The Frogs* Aristophanes calls the *Brekekekex, ko-ax, ko-ax,* "loud and long bubble-bursting accompaniment."

Most modern youths have koaxophilia. Particularly American youths. They are addicted to sound accompanying conversation, reading, learning. They do not listen to the sound, they merely hear it—their ears so accustomed to the river of sound that it flows by their conscious minds. Should the sound stop, they are immediately aware of an uncomfortable stillness. When loud, screaming jazz invades the silence they pursue their studies undisturbed in comfort. They sleep in comfort to the same accompaniment. This might well be a blessing in disguise. Today, when sirens scream you run to quiet howling dogs—not howling children.

See EREMIOPHOBIA

K RATION

Hated when issued, loved when needed.

In the last days, John Gilbert was seen everywhere with Marlene Dietrich. What did it mean to him? Was it an echo of the one great love?

L ADY

What every mother wants her daughter to be.

LAMB CHOPS VARIATION

For at least four or more people. Dutch oven. A bit of butter—just enough so nothing will stick.

First layer: Long, thin slices of onion to cover bottom.

Next layer: Lamb chops with salt and pepper.

Next layer: Potatoes in long, thin slices. Salt.

Next layer: Thin sliced onions.

Next layer: Lamb chops, salt, pepper, and so on and so on. You always finish with a thick layer of potatoes and some caraway seeds before you put on the lid. Medium flame on top of stove just to give a little starter, add broth to fill Dutch oven to a third, cover. Into oven, moderate heat. One hour or less. You have to test your meat. If your potato and onion slices have the right

91

thickness, meat, potatoes and onions should be done at the same time.

LANGUAGES

Learn them. Teach them to your children when they are very young. You cannot know the world, its problems, its ideals, its joys, its grief, or learn from other nations (let alone criticize them) if you do not speak their language.

First, learn the language thoroughly, then visit the country. Then judge—if you have to. Not the other way around. *See* JARGON

LAS VEGAS

I love that town. No clocks. No locks. No restrictions. No heavy hand of the law on your shoulder when you roll those dice.

LAUGHTER

There comes a time when suddenly you realize that laughter is something you remember and that *you* were the one laughing.

LAUGHTON, CHARLES

I wish he would have taught acting.

LAVENDER

Better on the bush than in the closet.

LEAD THROWING

A German custom, practiced on New Year's Eve.

The heated, liquid lead is thrown into a pail of cold

water, forming a solid mass into which each individual reads a meaning triggered by his own imagination. The most frequent shape are: ships, thrown mostly by men; cradles, thrown mostly by mothers. Those pieces that have no distinct shapes are the subject of much heated discussion. A wonderful pastime for the "letdown hour" directly following the ringing in of the New Year.

See NEW YEAR'S EVE

LEE, HARPER

To Kill a Mockingbird shook me up for a long time. I often think of the children as if they were real. I think of Atticus with the affection one has for the memory of someone one might have married had one known him then.

LEE, PEGGY

Honey-dripping singing, timing, phrasing; awakening no memories of other voices but awakening all senses to a unique feast.

LEFTOVERS

They are real fun. Take any boiled meat you have. Slice it. Fry onions with tomatoes, mushrooms if you have them, also sliced boiled potatoes, green peppers, plus any bits of cooked vegetables you might have; then add the meat, mix till all is hot, sprinkle with chopped parsley—and you will wish you had leftovers more often.

LEISURE

Robert Osborn's book. The best on the subject.

LETTERS

There is no excuse for not writing letters. My mother used to say:

"Don't tell me you have no time to write to someone who is waiting.

"There is a quiet place where no one disturbs you. You visit it every day—there you can write. You want to know what the place is? The emperor goes there on foot."

LETTERS (of Love)

Write them. Otherwise no one will know what wonderful feelings fill you. Even if the king or queen of your heart is unworthy (as you might have been told), write them—it will do you good. Keep copies.

LIAISON

A charming word signifying a union, not cemented and unromanticized by documents.

LIBRARY

The most precious of possessions.

LIFE

Life is not a holiday. Should you approach it thus, you will find holidays aplenty.

LIFE INSURANCE

When you lose your life, the insurance companies pay promptly in accordance with your policy. They cannot give you the endless third degrees: why, how, where did you lose it. They cannot confront you with the fact that they doubt you really lost it, or insinuate that you might have hidden it somewhere instead. They cannot refuse to insure you in the future because, having lost something, you are a "bad risk." It must be very frustrating for them. *See* INSURANCE

LILAC

Lilac bushes and the livin' is easy. The perfume can't be caught in bottles, which is just as well.

LILY OF THE VALLEY

In France, on the first day of May, you bring a bunch of lilies of the valley to your beloved; and you must be the first to do so or it's not true love.

LIMITATIONS

Know your limitations.

LINES (facial)

On men's faces they are called character—on women's—age.

LISTEN

You must listen all the time or you lose contact.

LIVER

A harassed liver is not only the reason for most headaches and pains in the neck, but also breeds a skeptical, sour outlook on life.

LIVERWURST

"The Consolation of the Sad."

Even when one is utterly miserable, unable to eat or think of food, it is easy to swallow. It not only stays down but, on the way there, tastes good. It will chase the stomach's butterflies away and also give a good push to the black clouds that make life seem too dark to bear.

LOGIC

I was brought up on Immanual Kant, the categorical imperative, and his teachings. ("The logical form of all judgement consists in the objective unity of the apperception of the concept which they contain.") Logic was demanded at all times. If there was no logic in my deductions, I was ruled out of any conversation. To this day I cannot get away from this strict adherence to logic, and I demand it now of others as it was demanded then of me.   *See* KANT, IMMANUEL

LOUIS, JEAN

Talent, knowledge, patience, kindness.

LOVE, 1

Love for the joy of loving, and not for the offerings of someone else's heart.

LOVE, 2

The lover's criterion is: I want you to be happy—but with me.   *See* MOTHER LOVE

LOVE, 3

Let him go—if he doesn't love you anymore.
Let her go—if she doesn't love you anymore.
                    See INDIFFERENCE

LOVE, 4

"Before you love
Learn to run through snow
Leaving no footprints."

This is a Turkish proverb. How clear the picture and how easily understood! *See* LOVE; MARRIAGE

LOVER'S LANE

The desire engendered in the male glands is a hundred times more difficult to control than the desire bred in the female glands. All girls agreeing to a lover's lane *tête-à-tête* in a car, knowing that they will limit their actions to arousing desire and then defend their "virtue," should be horsewhipped. *See* NECKING

LOYALTY

Should be one of the Commandments.

LUKEWARM

When this adjective applies to feelings, stop feeling whatever you are feeling.

*Marlene Dietrich as she appears in
"Around the World in 80 Days."*

MAGNETISM

You can read everywhere that the great scientists predict Mother Earth warming up enough to change New York into a Florida-like state climate-wise.

I, personally, look in vain for one of their statements finding the magnetic force of Mother Earth greatly increased *now*!

MAIL

The city of New York gives its private residents one mail delivery a day. If you post a letter in the afternoon you must send it special delivery in order to be certain it will be delivered the next morning. This condition makes New York something of a hick town.

MAILMAN

Let's all walk. They say that mailmen have no heart attacks.

MAKEUP

Too bad most of us need it.

MAKEUP MAN

The relationship between the makeup man and the film actor is that of accomplices in crime. They don't inform on each other, and they come to each other's rescue no matter what the danger. The makeup man is also the confidant of the actor. He is the one who knows the right number when he needs to awaken the actor who has overslept, which means he knows what numbers *not* to call.

MALE

He wants to be the prince who rides to rescue, to protect, to love the fairest of all women, nothing less. The images he has of this ideal woman are just the same the female has of the ideal man.

MANNERS

Good manners: Know your place.
Bad manners: Meddle.

MARBLES

Nothing will ever replace the joy of collecting and rolling them.

MARINES (U.S.)

I like that pride in their voices when they say it.

MARKET

Flower markets, fish markets, markets in wintertime,

charcoal stoves near each stand, farmers wearing three overcoats on top of each other, women with red apple-cheeks calling out their wares, their breath shooting into the grey air like steam from locomotives. . . .

MARRIAGE

There comes a moment when even the intelligent woman hears herself say: "I have given you the best years of my life."   *See* WIFE

MARRIED LOVE *(Strategy of)*

Love him. Unconditionally and with devotion.

You chose him. He must be wonderful.

If you chose him for any other reason, your problem, whatever it may be, lies in a realm of which I know nothing.

If your brain, instead of your heart, pilots your emotions, there must be regrets. You *cannot* trust your brain. You *can* trust your heart.

If you follow your heart there are no regrets, because there was no choice. Regretting is a fruitless, destructive occupation. Regretting, that is, what you did to yourself. Regretting the harm you did to others is a different matter. The feelings of others, particularly those of the man you live with, are very important. Much more important than your own.

You are a woman with a thousand little pockets in your being where you can tuck away little pains until tomorrow. A man hasn't got those pockets. His emotional system isn't quite as vast a labyrinth as yours. He is simpler, straighter than you are. This is not man's personal achievement, he is just made that way.

In order to love him well, you must try to be simpler, and straighter. This is much easier than it sounds. Just feel your way backward to the time when you first started to feel love. Before you started to play the game. Before you heard about and started to adopt the muddled values, tricks, the pride, the fencing, which make so many women lose their men.

You were young and felt love. This alone made you happy. The object of your love did not even have to belong to you. You were grateful if you could see him, and when he noticed you, your heart leaped. The fact that you loved him made your life wonderful. You didn't demand anything in those days—you wouldn't have dared. You just lived in a dream, and your hopes were humble. Just to be near him, you felt, was heaven. You did not think any further. The world was a beautiful place.

You had the optimism and the trust of youth. You were basically gay, with frequent melancholy hours, having the blues, or *Weltschmerz.*

Clara sings in Goethe's *Egmont:*
Cheering to heaven,
Saddened to death,
Happy alone
The soul that loves.

Youth is wise in matters of emotions. It takes the bad with the good in easy strides.

And then you grow up. You fall in love. Your heart leaps when he notices you. But now you want him for your own. At all times you and your heart wear your Sunday dress—and he falls in love with you. The world and life are wonderful.

But every day is not Sunday and you soon take off your Sunday dress. You and your heart. And somewhere back in your fairy-tale-hungry mind you are disappointed. And you think it must be somebody's fault. You "analyze," and find fault with the world. When you don't succeed in arriving at a fruitful conclusion you try to find the fault in a tangible object.

He does not necessarily have to be the reason. He just happens to be around when the constant Sundays become weekdays, with a few Sundays here and there and far apart, when you find out about life as you see it now in your weekday clothes. He knows too little about women and is too bewildered by your accusations to fence with half the skill you show. He thinks twice before he says words that might hurt you. You do not think at all. You find your target and you shoot. You have a vast supply of ammunition to draw on.

Your complaints range wide: from daily chores around the house and tired bones, to market prices, hot stoves, relatives, the neighbors—and the mink coat of your dreams.

He braves all your assaults because he loves you and wants peace. And for this peace and quiet that he wants, he soon trades in his age-old possession: his right to be the master of the house.

This is regrettable because you both are losers. The role of master of the house is not a lucky one for you if you obtained it by such unfair means. You lose your femininity. Let me again cite Goethe: "The eternal feminine draws us on." But you must be completely feminine, not just in bits and pieces and here and there where it fits the scheme of things.

To be completely woman you need a master, and in him a compass for your life. You need a man you can look up to and respect. If you dethrone him it's no wonder that you are discontented, and discontented women are not loved for long.

Your erstwhile king is loser too. His new role is unmanly and he knows it, but he resigns in hopes for armistice. Too bad for you if he discovers that indifference serves well as a shield against your whizzing arrows.

If you could stop and look at your battered target as a mother would or as a friend might do, you would not like the tactics you used—tactics you would not dare to use with anyone except the man you chose, the man whose love you want, to whom you said: "I want you for my own, forever after."

You were right in saying "forever after"—Cinderella-minded as you are. The fairy tale leaves you with the beautiful sentence about happiness forever after. But you forget that *before* it came to that poetic ending, there were dangers and sorrows and hardships. In real life, dangers and sorrows and hardships continue.

You face the bad ones together, the real sorrow and hardships. But only those. The other little sorrows, disappointments, annoyances, inconveniences you must face alone. Your sadness that has no apparent reason—face it alone and with yourself. It only proves that you are a sensitive, imaginative woman. Yield to it, it will pass more quickly that way. But don't try to find the reason in your present life, your man, your home, your routine chores of every day. Or even your duties to your children, if you are so blessed as to have them.

As our times "progress," women searching for a solution to emotional problems are steered further and further away from their own responsibility, and more and more into believing that others are responsible for their predicament. It is even becoming convenient to blame Mother for putting them the wrong way around into the cradle, or Father for doing something equally harmful to their future security.

This, to my way of thinking, has never solved anything. On the contrary, it tends to make those women more self-centered than they already are. It leads them further into complete preoccupation with themselves. Therefore, they cannot make someone else happy. Therefore, they are, themselves, unhappy.

To make a man happy is a full-time job. It leaves us very little time to take ourselves too seriously. And if you have children, you have no time at all. Or you *should* have no time at all. And when the work is directed toward the making and the keeping of a happy home, it makes you rich in contentment and puts occupational afflictions, like aching bones, into the only place where they belong, a hot bath.

This rich contentment will make you do a lot of things you had forgotten. You will remember your instinct's aerial, the tender, fine antennas you used to stretch his way in the beginning. Although neglected, they are still with you , dusty and bent, but you can straighten them. They'll help you know what he would like before he says it, as long ago when you were thrilled, and kissed, because you found another mystic link between your mind and his.

With your antennas at work, life should be easy. They'll tell you many things. His desires of each day and night and his dislikes. When to be quiet, when to talk, when to give an opinion on his problems and when just to listen, when to ask questions on how his work is going and when to wait until he wants to think of work and talk about it. When to welcome him with kisses, and when your hand in his for a moment is enough. If it was kisses you wanted, do not fret—you will be kissed, but later and surely better.

Do let him read the papers. But not while you accusingly tiptoe around the room, or perch much like a silent bird of prey on the edge of your most uncomfortable chair. (He will read them anyway, and he *should* read them, so let him choose his own good time.) Don't make a big exit. Just go. But kiss him quickly, before you go, otherwise he might think you are angry; *he is used to suspecting he is doing something wrong.*

Your antennas will make you wear the dress he likes and not the one he thinks too loud, too clinging, or too low in front. They'll tell you never to interrupt him while he is telling a story to friends, never to say, "Oh, that's not what happened, let *me* tell it." Tell your own stories if you have to talk, but leave his alone. And listen well, although you know his stories. He knows yours, too, and has to listen. Cherish the intimacy that your life together brings rather than dwell on the boring aspects. And continue to listen to your antennas. You will then not remark about his shortcomings or "the stupid thing he said this morning."

You will then, on the other hand, not (except in the company of your very closest and intimate friends) gloat over him, boast about his looks, his suits, his taste, his genius in all sorts of departments, and kiss him, hug or cuddle up to him in front of people. He is a man and it embarrasses him. People will know that you love him by the way you look at him, or by the way you take from his hand the glass he offers you.

Don't ever fight with him in public. There is nothing uglier than that. Wait till you are home, if fight you must. If he has hurt you, remember: Only the one you love can hurt you. But wait. Don't make your man impatient by crying, or accusing him of cruelty. Wait till you can think clearly, or you might say words too harsh or not quite to the point. It is more than possible that later you might not even want to mention it, or if you do you will be able to make your point much clearer. You'll find your man receptive only if there is no distortion of the facts, and if there's logic, most of all. Now, woman's logic is a muddled thing, as we all know. So all you have to do is think you are defending him against a woman and you will see your logic rise like Venus out of water, with your own love right there to give it a good leg up.

Your peace-loving antennas will make you stay at home when he is tired, when he prefers to look at baseball or at you (in moments when the game is dull) instead of twenty faces at a party. When the game is on, you can serve his dinner on a table so placed he doesn't have to strain his neck.

Don't make him do things. When he does them because he wants to do them, they'll be much better done. Let his timetable be *the* timetable.

Don't look upon him as a habit, or an object. The fact that objects like his bed, his comb, his toothbrush are with you can blind you into believing he cannot leave his bed, his toothbrush, comb, and you. He can, you know. And if he doesn't, but often has the thought that he would like to, you've lost him, even though you sleep beside him.

Your antennas tell you other things. To look for beauty and for joy in everything you do, instead of seeing all your daily duties drab and joyless (for which you need no effort). To clean your house and your machines that help you clean, and wash, and beat the eggs and mix the dough. To clean your children with your hands *(thank God there is no machine for that)*, dress them, go to the market which abounds in food so you can choose, push carriages or hold the hands of children on streets, in sunny parks, or sit on benches watching them play, walk home to feed them, make them rest. Then, in that quiet hour in your home, to feel the beauty of the day gone by, the joy in all the things you did, to start again the shorter afternoon, dress children, play, feed, wash them and listen for the sound of his key and the homecoming slam of the door.

Like the moon, the woman needs the man so she can shine and glow and put the tender silver into the strong reality of gold. The need to shine and glow makes her alive. Her tender presence will make the man want her as he wants sun and air. For what he dreams of is a tender woman who is at once a mother and a child.

See TENDERNESS

MARTINI

I am deeply suspicious of men who carry martinis to the lunch or dinner table.

MASSAGE

What a luxury! I never have time for it, but I'm for it.

MATERNITY BLUES

A modern state of mind. Modern in relation to "giving a name to everything." The state of mind might always have existed, I don't remember it though. As it is supposed to set in quite a few days after the birth of the baby, mothers used to be too busy to bother much with the blues. Take consolation, modern mothers, from Nietzsche, who spoke of the "melancholia of everything completed."

MATADOR

Courage and grace is a formidable mixture. The only place to see it is the bullring.

MAULDIN, BILL

On one of our meetings during the war, Hemingway looked at the crumpled edition of *Stars and Stripes* that had been wrapped around the bottle of Calvados and said: "This guy knows, but good."

MAY

The symbol of May is better than May.

MEAT

Never start cooking, frying, roasting or grilling meat when it comes out of the refrigerator. The best meat will remain tough and dry if you do that. Nothing disastrous happens to the meat when you take it out of the refrigerator an hour (at least) before you start preparing it. But, you can be sure that something disastrous happens to your dinner if you put cold meat into a grill, an oven or a pan. It will begin at once to give up its juice, because the heat cannot seal the juice in when the coldness of the meat makes the heat ineffective. Logical?

MEDALS

A great honour and joy to receive. If one has done something worth receiving a medal for, one should be duly proud and grateful. People claiming not to care about medals are just putting on airs.

MEDICAL ETHICS

They make me sick.   *See* HIPPOCRATIC OATH

MEDICAL MEN

People, before buying a car or a refrigerator, shop around for quite some time before deciding what to buy. If they would just use that same thoroughness when trusting their lives to a doctor, they would be better off.

MELANCHOLY

Having the blues, or *Weltschmerz*. Being in the depths of sadness is just as important an experience as being exuberantly happy.

MELODY

All the "sound," which in today's popular music and orchestrations is all-important, cannot replace the melody. Sounds will come and go. Melodies remain.

MEN'S CLOTHES

Black, midnight blue, dark blue, grey—for suits. Pale blue, pink, white—for shirts. Black, dark blue—for ties. Black—for shoes. Only Englishmen can wear brown rough suits and brown heavy-soled shoes and look elegant. Nobody else should try it.

MILK

I have my doubts about milk being necessary for the growing body. I was raised without milk, just because there wasn't any milk to give children. My teeth are fine, and my bones astound the specialists.

MINK *(Meaning mink coat)*

An American symbol. A luxury item with a quality rare in luxury items—toughness.

A badge of success for the giver as well as for the bearer. It provides the giver with proof of achievement, a clearly visible proof. It provides the bearer with a feeling of luxury, emotional security—also with warmth.

If a man can afford to buy mink—he should buy it. If he cannot—he should have compassion for his woman. One should not argue with a woman about the necessity of owning a mink. Symbols are necessary.

MISERY

"Misery Loves Company" the saying goes.

I, personally, don't long for company when I am miserable.   *See* GRIEF

MIXED DRINKS

Bad for you, and trouble for the barkeep.

MODESTY

It is easier for the unattractive girl to live a life of modesty.

See DEMAND AND SUPPY

MONEY

"Money, which represents the prose of life, and which is hardly spoken of in parlors without an apology, is, in its effects and laws, as beautiful as roses."

Ralph Waldo Emerson

Beautifully said. *See* ROSES

MOP

An implement falsely credited with cleaning floors. (Except in the hands of a sailor.)

MOROCCO

Looks better in films.

MOTHER

More solid than the ground under your feet when you are little, more solid than rock when you need to lean, and harder than rock when the leaning becomes a danger—when it's time for you to walk alone.

MOTHER LOVE

Love in its purest and most passionate form.

MOTHER'S DAY

Although it might have been invented by the United Florists as a business venture, let's be grateful to them in any case. It *does* remind neglectful sons and daughters to give a sign of life once a year.

A MOTHER'S HEART

There is a poem by Jean Richepin called "A Mother's Heart." Many people think it grotesquely sentimental. I don't. But here it is, in literal translation:

> There was once a poor fool who loved a young girl
> Long long long long ago
> But she pushed him away and said to him,
> Long long long long ago
> Bring me, I tell you, your mother's heart
> And give it to my dog.
> He went and slayed his mother
> Long long long long ago
> And took the heart, it was burning red
> He carried it and he stumbled and fell
> Long long long long ago
> And the heart rolled in the sand.
> He saw the heart roll in the dust
> Long long long long ago
> A cry was in the silent air
> The heart began to speak
> Long long long long ago
> Did you hurt yourself, my son?

MOTHER-IN-LAW

When you feel your wings grow, you are good at it.

See GRANDMOTHER

MOURNING

There is much to be said for the custom of wearing mourning clothes when a tragic loss has left you without strength. The widow's costume, particularly, inspires respect for sorrow, and the veil not only shadows her face but protects her from the glare of the gay life around her. A woman in mourning is treated gently at a time when she needs it most.

MUSHROOMS

In Europe there are many kinds of mushrooms. In America there is only one kind—the champignon, called mushroom. All mushrooms, mixed or single, cooked with a lot of dill and parsley and an onion, make the most delicious dinner with bread, their only companion.

See CHAMPIGNONS

MUSIC

How little time we working people have to listen to music, and what a loss this represents to our souls and our nervous systems.

Marlene Dietrich a n d her famed legs were seen in America for the first time in "Blue Angel," a German picture

DIETRICH ALWAYS HERSELF
Marlene Dietrich plays herself
in 20th-Fox's "Fate is
the Hunter," starring Glenn
Ford and Rod Taylor. Miss
Dietrich will be seen
entertaining World War 2
troops in New Guinea in a
brief sequence in the film.

N

AIL POLISH

Dark nail polish is vulgar.

NAKEDNESS

Easy for the beautiful, difficult for the ugly.

NAP

People who can nap are lucky. Don't disturb their napping just because you can't do the same.

NATIONALITY

Changing your nationality is not an easy step to take, even when you despise the beliefs and actions your country has adopted. Whatever you may tell yourself to the contrary, denying what you were brought up to cherish makes you feel disloyal. The love and respect for the country that is taking you in has nothing to do with it.

NECKING

A dirty pastime.

NEGLIGEE

The thing you hopefully buy when you first get married and which you wish you could return when your eyes encounter it crowding your closet while you grab for your workclothes year in and year out.

NEGLIGENCE

Unforgivable. *See* IGNORANCE

NEUROTIC

The more plentiful the work, the less time to be neurotic.

NEW YEAR'S EVE

Gaiety, champagne, hope.

See OPTIMISM; LEAD THROWING

NICE AND EASY

The nicest way of doing things.

NIGHTCLUB

I like the genuine Russian ones in Paris where one can cry over the *Little Cornflower* with sobbing violins for company. Fashionable nightclubs do not attract me.

NOBILITY

"Unwillingness to renounce or share our responsibilities." *Nietzsche*

My parents taught me never to renounce or share my responsibilities.

NOLI ME TANGERE

This expression has two meanings: "Touch me not" and "Don't interfere." Both are sayings after my own heart.

NORMAL

We all have quite definite ideas about what is normal. Let's stick to those ideas and let psychiatry keep its definitions of modern man out of our vocabulary. We need some norms to go by in order to communicate without misunderstanding.

NOUVEAU RICHE

He enjoys his new riches far more than the "ancien riche." His joy is dampened somewhat by his ignorance in matters of behaviour and manners. They don't come wrapped with the riches.

NUN

The most beautiful poem by my favorite poet: "Nun's Lament." *See* RILKE, RAINER MARIA

With JVS at the time of the lawsuit

Oasis

The bookshop on Fifty-second Street and Fifth Avenue in New York which stays open till midnight.

OBJECTIVE

Contrary to general belief it is possible to be completely objective about one's own accomplishments and deeds.

OFFSPRING

Your offspring, at a certain age, will reproach you for everything you have ever done for them. Thumbs will be down on every decision you ever made in their behalf.

Don't argue, and don't try to whitewash yourself from your sins. It will pass. It's like the measles. The only thing for which you will receive something resembling a pat on the back is your insistence on the study of languages. *That* they will forgive.   See LANGUAGES

OIL

That wonderful substance the other fellow gets rich on.

OMELETTE ÉCUME

When you are stuck for a dessert, this is it. Takes no time at all.

2 yolks of eggs per person. Mix with 3 tablespoons of sugar till creamy. Beat the whites stiff. Fold one into the other carefully, so the whites don't fall. Heat a tablespoon of butter, or more, golden in a large frying pan. Pour mixture slowly into the pan. Turn flame low. Very low. Cover pan. Wait. After a couple of minutes, you can peek. When the omelette is thickening on the rim of the pan, try lifting it with a dull knife, enough to see if it is browning well underneath. But do that only if the omelette can be lifted a bit. Otherwise wait some more seconds. If it browns too much, turn your flame a trifle lower. The top should look as before, but it should be warm. The bottom of the omelette should be golden brown. When this is accompished, put the platter on which you want to serve the omelette near the pan. Slide omelette onto the platter—it should just glide over if you used enough butter—and when half of it is on the platter, tilt the pan so that the other half folds over the first, sandwiching in the yellow foam. This has to be eaten right away, so don't ever start it when your guests are still eating the main course. Let them smoke and have coffee while you are making this.

ONASSIS, ARISTOTLE

One rich man who was not dull.   *See* RICH

OPHIR, SHAI K.
>Once he must have been a thoroughbred horse.

OPTIMISM
>Have it. There is always time to cry later.

ORDER
>I need it. Emotionally and physically.

ORDINARY
>I dislike people who start sentences with: "I'm just an ordinary human being."

ORGANIZATION
>Organization is speed's best helpmate.

ORIFLAMME *(Red banner split at one end to form flame-shaped streamers. Early French kings' military ensign.)*
>My heart is that for France.

OSTEOPATHY
>The dogma of this science is the most logical of all. The A.M.A. considers osteopathy to be a cult (1961 Convention Report).　　　　　　　　　　　　　　*See* CHARLATAN

OWE
>Too many women believe that "the world owes you something," "you have a right to possessions, amusements, luxuries, etc.," and more of those treacherous promises. That kind of thinking tends to endow those women with a lazy expectancy of the good things to fall into their

laps—including being loved and honored and respected by a man. Good things don't fall that easily, and the lazy expectancy soon changes into disappointment, bitterness and other frustrating emotions.

See FRUSTRATION

OXYGEN *(out of a tank)*

Why wait till you are under a tent to breathe it in?

OZONE

I adore the smell of it.

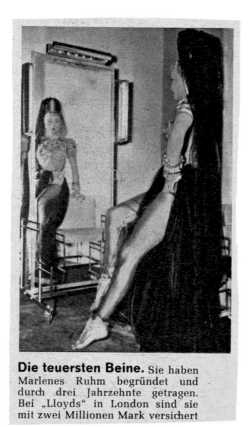

Die teuersten Beine. Sie haben Marlenes Ruhm begründet und durch drei Jahrzehnte getragen. Bei „Lloyds" in London sind sie mit zwei Millionen Mark versichert

P<small>ANTS</small>

In Texas, when you want to say that a man is beautiful or handsome you simply say: "His pants fit him."

PARALLEL

"Two parallel lines meet at infinity." The first law of geometry (non-Euclidean, of course) to start me dreaming.

PARIS

Home which keeps its promise.   *See* FRANCE

PARIS-MATCH

The ultimate in magazine journalism.

PARLEZ-MOI D'AMOUR

Yes, please do. The loving heart is a bad mind reader.

PARQUET FLOORS

The old ones are works of art. I shave the ordinary ones, stain them dark and wax and polish them regularly. Another one of those housework occupations providing immediately visible results. *See* HOUSEWORK

PASSION

"Tenderness is the repose of passion." *Joseph Joubert*

See TENDERNESS

PATCEVITCH, I. V. A.

My description of gentlemen and cavaliers is not valid in his regard. If I could really describe him and all his qualities he would be embarrassedly resentful and would accuse me of being indiscreet.

PATIENCE

Patience can become second nature, if taught early enough. One of those gifts to your children for which you will be hated first and loved later.

PATTON, GENERAL GEORGE S.

He never flattered or praised me. He gave me orders and the nature of the assignment conveyed the trust he chose to repose in me.

PEACE

Why does it elude us so frequently, when it is so sincerely desired?

PEDIATRICIANS

I love them all. They love children. They help children.

There are no answers to their questions. They read a baby's eyes, an art long neglected and discarded by doctors. He puts a naked ear on a baby's stomach and the awareness of the delicacy of his patient makes his face tender however serious it may be. He never has the horrible poker-face that adults have to look at when waiting for the doctor's verdict. They know more about nutrition than nutritionists. They call a spade a spade and a rash a rash. They concentrate on the patient. One at a time. They set their minds to *not evoke fear*. Their hearts must be big, sweet lollipops.

PENCIL SHARPENER *(Electric)*

Anyone who doesn't have one misses a great delight.

PHILIPE, GERARD

The perfect actor. Mentally and physically. The personification of a romantic image. I saw him in *Caligula* (by Camus) when he was just starting. Thunderstruck, tongue-tied, shaking with excitement, I waited to see him in front of his dressing-room door. I am certain that he took me for a crazy film actress, although he behaved beautifully during the few embarrassing moments when I told him of his greatness. His death hurt me very much, not because I felt a physical loss, but because with him went the tangible image of the romantic ideal behind the footlights.

PHOTOGRAPHY

Photography should be listed and respected as a science. It can not only create—but create wonders. It can make midgets out of giants and giants out of midgets in more ways than one.

PHYSICAL LOVE

Any society that allows conditions to exist in which the adolescent begins to connect guilt with physical love raises a generation of defectives.

PIAF, EDITH

The sparrow of the Paris streets. A waif from the wrong side of the tracks. A soul which was born hurt and wouldn't say die. An idealist, an optimist with sad eyes, a frail body marked by a childhood full of hunger, hands of a princess. Delicate and robust, courageous and shy, singing her heart out, giving her love, her friendship, her help and inspiration, believing in all and everything with the mighty strength of her romantic soul—the sparrow become Phoenix.

PIANO

A home without a piano is waiting for something.

PIE

There is no better pie than lemon chiffon pie.

PILOT

A man who should be warmly and politely thanked when he has landed a plane in which you are a passenger.

POLITENESS

Easy to learn. Easy to practice.

POSSESSION

A man's age-old possession: his right to be master of the house.

POSSESSIVENESS

Possessiveness, the beautiful, heartless imposter! It glitters almost as if it were love. It is destructive, and the most treacherous of shiny hooks that have been thrown to sea to hook a man. If you are a clever fisherwoman, know the winds, the tides, the moon, you will hook him. But he will struggle. You will use your skill to hold the line, not to have it break, to get him good and tired, to pull him in. And finally you take him off the hook, bleeding and hating you. You throw him on the bottom of your boat, feeling kind, like Florence Nightingale, because there is a pool of water there, and watch him as he beats the boards, all dazed and dumb. And then you wonder what to do with him. By that time, if he lives, or if he is a crazy, mixed-up fish and doesn't hate you, you have no longer any use for him. You proved it to yourself that you are stronger, and therefore sport and game are at an end.

If you have any heart you throw him back into the sea; his wounds will heal and scars might be reminders and a lesson. And if you don't, you will regret it all too soon. You didn't love him, but you wanted love. It doesn't work that way. A man needs time to see the difference between possessiveness and love. When you least expect it he'll see the light. The hurt that you feel then is not your aching heart, it is your aching vanity.

See VANITY

POTATOES

I love them. I eat them.

POT-AU-FEU *(Boiled Beef)*

You don't have to be a cook to do this well. Get the right kind of meat. If you know a French butcher, you are safe. If you don't, get: Beef shank center cut and cross ribs, topside or silverside. Lean meat cannot be used. If you have a large family, this dish is ideal, because you can serve it two nights in a row, and if there is any meat left over, you can make a third dinner by cutting the meat in slices and frying it with sliced onions and potatoes.

Into a large pot you put at least 4 pounds of the meat, 2 large onions, a couple of leeks, 2 large carrots, a celery root, a large bunch of parsley, the last you take out after an hour of cooking. Salt, peppercorns. Add enough water to cover. Bring to boil. Turn flame low and cook 2 to 3 hours, or until your meat is juicy and tender. Remove the white foam which forms on the water from time to time. Strain and put the meat back into the broth.

Into individual pots you put some of the broth in which you cook: potatoes, carrots (left whole), small white onions, white cabbage. Use a bit of water with the broth for the onions and the carrots so as not to waste too much of your broth. The broth in which you cooked the potatoes you pour back into the main broth once the potatoes are done. Just leave a bit of broth on them to keep them hot. The cabbage needs very little broth and water, as cabbage gives out water while cooking. If you do not have much time, you can steal broth from the main pot after the first hour of cooking.

Serve the meat on a large platter, surrounded by the vegetables, alternating them to fit the shape of the platter. Sprinkle very generously with finely chopped parsley all over everything.

Put coarse salt and freshly grated horseradish on the table. Put some parsley in the soup bowls too before you pour the broth into them. Serve it before or with the main course.

If you are a student of French cookbooks, you will read that chicken and turnips are part of the *pot-au-feu*. The reason I omit them and cook all the vegetables separately: I like the broth of the *pot-au-feu* to retain the pure taste of meat.

POUTING
I hate it, but men fall for it, so go on and pout.

POWER POLITICS
Boys playing: You-show-me-yours, I-show-you-mine.

PRESLEY, ELVIS
He arrived on the scene when the young needed a romantic image. He filled the bill, and on top of that he could sing. And he had the sound of today.

PRESS CLIPPINGS *(Your own)*
Only fools keep them.

PRIDE
In love, pride is not as dangerous to men as it is to women. A man forgets his pride when pride is not the issue.

See VANITY

PRIVACY *(Personal)*

A man's good right.
I insist on mine—
I fight if necessary, and would gladly
kill opponents.

PRODUCERS

The extraordinary "creative" producer (creative in deference to the producer in name only) is a man who, after deciding on the work he wants to produce, chooses the ideal collaborator for each job in connection with the planned production. He then proceeds to interest these men in his plan and convince them of the necessity of their collaboration. Once they have agreed on the basic ideas, the producer leaves them alone so that they can create and use their talents to the fullest extent.

The ordinary producer operates differently. Once the contracts have been signed, he imposes his ideas from the construction of the work to the casting, costuming, etc., and meddles in everybody's functions. He complains about the stubborness, stupidity, the uncooperative spirit of his erstwhile heroes, who do not throw in the towel *only* because of their devotion to the cause and the job they feel compelled to finish.

PROPERTY MAN

The property man attached to a film in the making is always a man with a twinkle in his kind eyes. Not that he is picked for such qualities. It just so happens that all property men are lovable people. The property man's function is the supplying of props that are being used in the film. He houses them all in a cart. This cart is like a magician's box. Besides the objects demanded by the script it can produce a vast array of articles that have no relation whatsoever to the film in the making. But the property man knows too well the sudden turns creative minds can take and is not gong to get caught with his magic box down. As anticipation is his middle name, he can cook and he can serve the perfect dinner for an intimate *tête-à-tête*. He is never tired, never weary. He peps up his favorites with jokes and coffee and the secret drink to ease the strain when work is almost done. Then, when the order of "wrap 'em up" has sounded, he closes up his cart much like a coachman gently throws a blanket on his sweating horse.

PSYCHIATRY

I bow respectfully to this science.

PUNISH

The only persons permitted to punish children should be persons who love them.

PURITANS

"The Puritans nobly fled from a land of despotism to a land of freedom, where they could not only enjoy their own religion, but prevent everybody else from enjoying his." *Charles F. Browne.*

Q

UACK

Not everyone called a quack is a quack—except quacks and ducks.

QUALITY

There is nothing better.

See DRESS; SHOES; GLASS SLIPPER; ROLLS-ROYCE

QUARREL

There should be a law against it.

QUARTZ

Rose-quartz cut in the shape of a heart is the prettiest jewel a little girl can wear.

QUEEN

Being a Queen must entail enormous minuses and very few pluses.

QUESTIONS

If they are personal, don't ask them.

QUIT

Don't, if the goal is at all attainable. You won't like yourself in the morning if you do. *See* GOETHE

QUOTATIONS

I love them because it is a joy to find thoughts one might have, beautifully expressed with much authority by someone recognizedly wiser than oneself.

Above: In *The Blue Angel*
Below: In *Three Loves* (with Fritz Kortner)

R

ADIGUET, RAYMOND

His masterpiece: *Le Diable au corps.*

See PHILIPE, GERARD

RADIO

A great medium; and I won't let anyone bury it yet.

RAIMU

Tragedian and comedian. In my book, the greatest actor.
The scene in the flower bin in *La Femme du Boulanger*
—a gem of portraying opposed emotions in a few short
minutes.

RECIPES

The recipes I am including here are easy to make. As I
have only learned to cook what I like, there is nothing
"fancy" I can share with you. Also, as I am addressing

myself to women (or men) who know the elements of cooking, I will not give basic measures, as cookbooks do, or tell you exactly how many people you can serve. I usually give the minimum, and you can be safe in surmising that two people will be well served. As I cook by eye, I simply don't know measurements. I will try though not to be too vague.

RED

It is not very wise to buy a red dress. But I can understand the temptation—simply because men will say: "Who is the girl in the red dress?"

RED CROSS

During my war years, whenever in need of luxury items we were sure to find them with the Red Cross personnel.

REFRIGERATOR

A great hygienic invention, but only too often the enemy of the cook.   *See* MEAT

REFUGEE

All refugees have my deep sympathy. To lose one's fatherland by necessity or by choice is a tragedy. (Except if the choice is prompted by the desire to escape taxes.)

REGRET

Immunity to regret lies in adherence to a strict code of conduct consistent with mortal laws. Moreover, it must also be consistent with those laws one considers noble and complete and which could stand alone should mortal laws cease to exist.

REINHARDT, MAX

Not much is done today that he did not do first, and much is called new today that he had forgotten.

See STANISLAVSKI

RELAX

Commonly used in America, even by children. Outside of America only used when suggested to people who have really done something.

REMARQUE, ERICH MARIA

The last of the romantics.

Besides the great writer that he was, he had a capacity few men have.

The capacity to understand the emotions of all living creatures.

Understand them and soothe aching hearts, including mine, all through the years of his self-chosen exile in America.

He never showed his despondence over the loss of his native language.

Maybe, having me as a lucky receptacle, I was of some use to him. *See* COURAGE

RESISTANCE

Antoine de Saint-Exupéry, the articulate voice of France during the dark years of Nazi occupation.

RESONANCE

Every man needs a resonance. A woman who loves a man should be content to be just that.

RESTAURANT

You will know the first-class restaurant by the way the food is served, without you and your friends being questioned as to who ordered what.

RETURN

To return to the pastures of one's youth is easy, but always sad. As one cannot return to one's youth, the pastures evoke melancholy rather than joy.

RETURN TICKET

Don't ever succumb to the desire to change it for cash when you are far away from home.

REVENGE

Revenge is a logical act of a defeated people. The victor who does not count on this logical fact is just plain idiotic.

RHYTHM

You have to be born with it.

RICE

Fill the pot with cold water, enough to double the amount of rice. Add a small onion cut in half, a small piece of butter and salt, cover the pot. Once the water boils, turn flame very, very low. When the water has disappeared, the rice should be just right, not too soft. Do not stir or turn the rice. You can look at it once in a while to check if there is still liquid in the pot. If you have miscalculated your amount of water and the rice is done before all the water is gone, leave the lid off the pot and leave the pot a little while longer on the very low fire. Take the onion out before serving. If you want to reheat rice, always do it in a double boiler.

RICH

Most rich people are pretty dull.   *See* EARNING

RICHTER, SVIATOSLAV

A once and only event which repeats itself.

RICKETS

The absence of rickets amongst the poor and improperly nourished children—the triumph of vitamin D. Doubting Thomases, take note!   *See* VITAMINS

RILKE, RAINER MARIA

My idea of a poet. He has been translated into English—that is, *attempts* have been made to translate his poems. It is impossible to translate the beauty of his style, but all attempts are worth it. His thoughts have never before been thought and nobody wrote, writes, or will write as he did.

RIVIERA

Don't be blase and say it's too crowded. Go and find another spot like it!

ROAST CHICKEN

Young chickens. Dutch oven.

Rub the chickens with the juicy side of half an onion. Salt. 1/8 pound of butter and one cup of chicken broth, or, if you don't have any, one cup of water. Into the Dutch oven. Heat on top of the stove. Put in the chickens. Cover. Into the oven. Medium heat. In about fifteen minutes you start basting the chickens. Each time you find the liquid nearly gone add a bit of cold water or broth and scrape the brown crust from the bottom of the pan and from the sides into the liquid. Never add a lot at a time. Keep on basting till you find the chickens to be tender to the delicate touch of a kitchen fork. Baste again and take off the lid of the Dutch oven. Turn the heat up. The chickens are done; they have only to brown now. *Stay in the kitchen* and baste every five minutes. When you like the colour, take the Dutch oven out of the stove. If you want the chickens to be crisp when they are eaten, better have dinner at once, otherwise, when you cover them to keep them hot, the crispness will go. After you put the chickens on the platter, put the Dutch oven on the top of the stove, flame high. Add water and scrape off all brown crusts from the bottom and sides before pouring the gravy over the chickens. Rice and green salad or tiny peas go best with this. I hope you remember to have the chickens room temperature when you start, and please remove the strings with which they are tied up.   *See* MEAT

ROCKING CHAIR

"The rocking chair will get me."

I wish it would. Preferably on a sunny porch in Wisconsin.

ROLLS-ROYCE

It's not an illusion, it's reality.

ROME

Most of us city dwellers open our windows onto dreary views *if* we open them at all. The Romans not only open them, but every nook and cranny of their town is beautiful. What fools we are, we, who don't live there.

See ITALIA

ROOM SERVICE

If only the waiter would not stand around waiting for you to sign the check, forcing you to get out of bed, shower or bathtub, to put on clothes, to interrupt long-distance or local calls—if only he would let you have your morning cup of coffee in privacy!

ROOSEVELT, ELEANOR

"There is a certain blend of courage, integrity, character and principle which has no satisfactory dictionary name. . . ." *Louis Adamic*

ROSES

I like them best freshly cut from the garden. The blonde ones with the tender, drooping stems smell as a rose should smell.

ROSSELLINI, ROBERTO

I met him one evening and found myself the next day typing his manuscript in a cold cellar apartment of a writer who also had met him only the night before (after running all over Paris to track him down).

Such was his gift to find not only enthusiastic but useful disciples. Among his many gifts he had one rare one: He was a friend.

RUSSIANS

I love Russians for their sense of humour, their passionate souls, their nonbourgeois hearts. Their spiritual range is wide. They can swing down to the depths and up to lofty heights, never stopping in the safe middle section of lukewarm emotions.

This was the impression I formed through their literature. It was confirmed when I met Russian people in all walks of life.

RUSSIAN SALAD *(One of them)*

Sliced apples, sliced tomatoes, sliced onions. Salt. Children like it without dressing. You can add oil and lemon, but no other kind of salad dressing. Serve it in large bowls. Makes a very good dinner with nothing else but cheese, bread and butter.

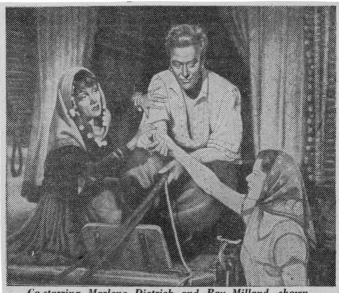

Co-starring Marlene Dietrich and Ray Milland, shown here with Roberta Jonay. Next Wednesday is opening day

SACRIFICE

The best measuring cup of your love.

SADNESS

Bitter in childhood, sweet in adolescence, tragic in old age.

SAFETY

"Better put a strong fence 'round the top of the cliff,
Than an ambulance down in the valley."

Joseph Malines

Let all grandmothers quote this when they are accused by their children of being too much concerned with their grandchildren's safety.

SAGITTARIUS

Straight shooters, radiant, vital, creative, idealistic, unconventional, stubborn in beliefs which are usually sincere.

SALAD DAYS

It is recklessness of feeling we deplore losing. We become so bloody sensible and nice.

SALE

The temptation of getting things "cheaper" is cluttering up our households with unnecessary objects and actually burdens the budget.

SALK, DR. JONAS

He has a shrine in this mother's heart.

See SWIMMING POOL

SANDWICH

A wonderful invention for all people like myself who like to eat on the run.

SATIN

A deceptive fabric. It looks good enough to eat when it is spread out, but made into a dress it transfers its shiny quality to the bearer and spreads her out. There are some beautifully clinging unshiny satins in France for long evening dresses. Difficult to find even in the land of silk.

SATURN

The celestial taskmaster. He won't let you get away with anything.

SCHMALZ

A melted fat used a lot for frying, roasting, and cooking in Austria, Germany, Hungary. It has different names in different countries. But fat is used all over Europe instead of butter, which is expensive, browns much faster, and therefore invites burning. Back fat and leaf lard of pork are the two components. Cut it in squares, put it into a high pot, add a sprig of thyme, a sprig of marjoram, one onion, and cover. Simmer slowly until all squares are melted evenly. Strain into an earthen bowl and cool. If you don't have to watch your cholesterol, try it thinly spread on rye bread with salt. Children love it. I swoon over it just like I swoon over schmaltzy music.

SCHNITZEL

If you can flirt your butcher out of real pink baby veal you can make schnitzels. He must cut slices not thicker than a quarter inch from the best part of the thigh (the filet of veal also called fricandeau). *You* pound them into further thinness. Don't tear them, but pound them.

Beat an egg with a fork to mix the yellow with the white. Add salt and a bit of pepper (finely ground). Put on large plate. Put bread crumbs on another. Season the bread crumbs with a little salt and pepper. (Don't forget that you already have some salt in the egg.) Put plenty of butter (or oil) into a frying pan that can house the schnitzels comfortably. Even crowding them is better than frying them in too large a pan. Put your plates under hot, running water to warm them. (Yes, you can put them in the electric plate warmer.) Quarter a lemon. Put the finishing touches on the vegetables you plan to serve. Put a piece of brown paper on an empty spot on your kitchen table. You might need it. Take a look if your customer or customers are ready to have dinner or have finished their first course. Only then flip on the flame under the pan. Not *all* the way. Lay the first schnitzel into the eggs. Turn it over gently. Move it over to the plate that holds the crumbs, turn it over and over till the crumbs cover the meat everywhere. Your butter should be golden brown by now. Lay the schnitzels carefully into the hot butter. Turn the flame up. This will seize the crumbs and give them body. Lower the flame after a short minute to medium. Turn schnitzels over to fry the other side the same way. While the other side is frying, dry your plates and line them up. When you lift out each schnitzel the crust should not be soggy and dripping. But if it is, lay it for a second, yes, you said it, onto the brown paper. Do not pour any of the butter remaining in the pan onto the schnitzel. A real (wiener) schnitzel should be dry. Put a quarter of lemon on the plate and a sprig of parsley if you have it handy. If you serve any vegetable that has juice, don't put it on the same plate. No use wetting your schnitzel when it should be dry. But don't scold anyone who puts everything on the same plate. As long as you serve it dry, *your* conscience is clear. *They* are their own bosses.

SCHOOLS

I am against coeducational schools. Boys have enough to cope with without girls adding to the disturbance mentally and physically.

SCHOPENHAUER

His world was highly romantic, which appealed to me,

and he was a realist, which balanced all. *The World as Will and Idea* was *the* book for me for quite a number of my formative years. *See* GOETHE

SCOFIELD, PAUL

I saw him at a time when most actors and stars affected the head-scratching, incoherent mumbling, embarrassed attitude on screen and stage. He played a dual role perfectly in *Ring Round the Moon*. And I almost fell off my seat with delight. He knew which foot to put forward, he had authority and elegance, he had perfect diction, handled a cape with great skill; in other words, he seemed to be like John Barrymore had been described to me. From then on I did not feel cheated anymore for having missed Barrymore.

SCORPIO

The world, the flesh and the devil.

SEASONS

Necessary and beautiful. My biggest loss when I had to live in Hollywood.

SECRET

One should think twice before burdening a good friend with a secret.

SEDUCE

Anyone who was seduced wanted to be seduced.

SELF-DISCIPLINE

The most useful of all disciplines.

SELF-SERVICE

Self-service is labelled "progressive." The only progress I can see is that the customer does the work of the employees who have been ousted. This is progress? If the goods the customer purchases are cheaper because of this self-service, there is some logic to the proceedings. It also keeps the customer happy, who does not care whose stomach may go empty as long as it isn't his own.

See TELEPHONE

SENTIMENT

In fear of being sentimental people often shun sentiment. A sad confusion.

SERMON *(Funeral)*

If you believe what the man says, how can you cry? How can you say, "Poor Jack died"? How can you cry when everything on this earth is sheer misery compared to the glory that awaits him? If you believe what the man says.

SERVICE STRIPES

They should be adopted by civilian concerns for their long-term employees.

SEX

In America an obsession. In other parts of the world a fact.

SHAW, GEORGE BERNARD

He cabled me once: "When you come to Europe call on me to discuss the *Millionairess* film, or call anyhow just for fun. Cable address Socialist, London."

We spent a long afternoon in a sundrenched room
and he showered his wit on me, generous gentleman
that he was.

SHAW, IRWIN

"I got a religion that wants to take heaven out of the
clouds and plant it right here on the earth where most
of us can get a slice of it." From *Bury the Dead*.

SHOES

Shoes are more important than suits and dresses. Good
shoes give elegance to your entire appearance. Buy one
pair of good shoes instead of three pairs of bad quality.

See FEET

SILVER DOLLAR

I love silver dollars. They feel like real money.

SINATRA

One of the most gentle of all the men I know.

SINS OF OMISSION

The blackest of our daily sins.

SLANG

Slang has vision, imagination, gallows humour and man-
ages defiantly *épater le bourgeois*.

SLEEP

Something holy.

SLEEPING ALONE

Sleeping alone, except under doctor's orders, does much harm. Children will tell you how lonely it is sleeping alone. If possible you should always sleep with someone you love. You both recharge your mutual batteries free of charge.

SLEEPING POTION *(Without prescription)*

On your way home stop at a delicatessen store and ask for a sardine-and-onion sandwich on rye bread. Eat it when you have finished your evening chores. You will just have enough time to wash and brush your teeth before slumber overtakes you.

SMILE

Smile when you feed a baby. Smile till your face hurts. He will connect food with joy. A bottle-fed baby does not have the advantage of a breast-fed baby. A nursing mother smiles with every pore of her being when she looks down on her child.

SOFT DRINKS

The gooey, bubbly sea drowning our American children.

SOLITUDE

Sounds more elegant and detached than loneliness, but it's the same.

SON

Your son isn't your son for life—if he is normal.

See DAUGHTER

SOPHISTICATE

The word seems to have changed its meaning in today's usage. To me it signifies something not genuine, not honest. I never use the word, for that reason.

SORROW

Respect for sorrow is a natural instinct. But under the mantle of on-the-spot reporting, people in the throes of great tragedy are being cruelly imposed upon by reporters and photographers lacking nothing but taste and imagination.

SOUND MEN *(Film)*

They serve two masters without their nerves showing. Sometimes they have to cope with a third one: the actor who simply cannot raise his voice a fraction of a breath without surfacing out of the depth of his great acting.

See FILM CUTTER

SOUP

At certain times soup is the ideal food. Soup not only warms you and is easy to swallow and to digest, it also creates the illusion in the back of your mind that Mother is there.

SPACE PROBING

My feeling about this vast endeavor of man is expressed in a poem by Friedrich von Schiller:

The Diver

". . .Ah! happy ye who live in this rosy light!
It is awful yonder beneath the sea!
To tempt the Gods can never be right,

I warn you, to be so bold
As to seek what the Gods in their mercy withhold."

SPAIN

The most romantic of all countries.

SPELLING

Many Americans, graduated from college or even holding university degrees, are unable to spell correctly and
they are not the slightest bit embarrassed. In Europe,
any eighth-grader unable to spell correctly would not
only be ineligible for high school but also would be the
disgrace of the family.

STAGE FRIGHT

I have no sympathy with actors trembling in the wings.
They have chosen acting as their profession; let them
get on with it.

STAMINA

Ideals are the best food for stamina and superhuman
endurance.

STANISLAVSKI, KONSTANTIN

Being a Reinhardt student I am not without prejudice
toward the teachings of Stanislavski. (Although however
different their approaches, the final quality of performance was their common aim.) The interpretation of
Stanislavski's methods, practiced in America, is concentrated mainly on one aspect of his teachings, and the
main aim is concentrated more on the approach the actor
has to the part than the final performance. Any ideas I

might have had about the importance of the actor's approach to a part were extinguished for good when Max Reinhardt, sitting in the empty theatre, listened to my prayer of Gretchen in *Faust*. When I got up from my knees embarrassedly brushing off the dust from my skirt, his voice rang out: "You did not make me cry." I lifted my tearstained face and said: "But, Professor, I am crying!" The answer was: "I do not care if you cry or laugh or what emotion you harbor, your task is to make me cry, me, the spectator. I couldn't care less what *you* feel! Make *me* feel!" *See* JOUVET

STATIONERY STORE

People who adore stationery stores are like dope addicts about paper clips, paper clamps, Gem clips, ring clips, bulldog clips, Magic Markers, china markers, felt-tip pens, Scotch tapes, Mystik tapes, masking tapes, varieties of pads, notebooks with spirals on tops, notebooks with spirals on the side, short, long, wide, narrow. Paper devoted to erasers, paper—thick, stiff, hard, soft, rough, large like canvas, surfaces like linen or pigskin. The addict buys feverishly all he needs and all he does not need and has absolutely no use for. He just cannot leave it in the store.

I remember buying the most beautiful pale blue legal paper, which felt like silken blotting paper, in a village stationery store in Haddonfield. I look at it once in a while and it definitely sends me.

See HARDWARE STORE

STEAK

If an American raves about a wonderful dinner he had

the night before, you don't have to look into a crystal ball to know what was served.

STERNBERG, JOSEF VON

The man I wanted to please most.

STRAVINSKY

Le Sacre du Printemps is the most erotic music I know.

STUPIDITY

The only defect with which I lose my patience.

SUAVE

I can get along very well without the use of this word.

SUET PUDDING

The manna of my childhood, prepared with great ritual by English governesses.

SUGAR

The root of great evil. Give children honey instead.

SUN

Mothers and nurses have the firm belief that the last rays of an autumn sun finding its way through intervals in the endless array of many storied buildings, have an extraordinary power, fortifying their babies. You can see them crowding the carriages, turned towards the sun, rocking them gently; then dispersing, whispering good-byes, wheeling against the wind, satisfied to go home in the darkened streets.

SUNSPOTS

I remember a day when all telephonic and all cable connections to Europe were halted by sunspots playing havoc with the inventions of men.

SUPERIORITY

If you have it, don't show it unless it is constructive.

SUPERSTITION

Superstitions are habits rather than beliefs. Often one abides by them not prompted by conviction but by a memory of cherished indications that grown-ups were not unwavering in their sureness after all. The memory of the hand that pulled you back to let the black cat pass, the voice that said, "Come here, don't walk under that ladder," or, "There is a new moon, make a wish," brings into focus another cherished thought: The hands, the voices all belonged to people who wished you well. Little wonder then, your reluctance to break the chain of habit, even when the belief is gone.

SWIMMING POOL

I would like to suggest that all public swimming pools put up a small statue of Dr. Jonas Salk on the grounds surrounding the pools. It would remind the mothers and fathers watching their children jump and swim who is responsible for their peace of mind.

See SALK, DR. JONAS

SYMBOL

To each his own. Symbols are necessary.

See MINK

T ACT

There are people who have a natural built-in tact of the heart. If you know of one, treat him gently; they are hard to come by.

But tact can be taught; best when we are young, and not by words but by example.

TALLEYRAND

The French statesman who said: "A married man will do anything for money.

TARRAGON

The delicious! Puts the *Made in France* label on your salad.

TAURUS

It is very good to be a Taurus. For the Taurus I mean. To live with a Taurus is not very easy. Don't ever argue with a Taurus, it is just as well to agree with him right away. He is easy to handle with love and affection. He needs security, emotional and material; he does not analyze, he lives by instinct. Once he has decided that you and the home you make are essential, he is the most faithful of men.

TAXI DRIVERS

They and I reminisce shortly on short rides, long on long rides, but there is no ride without reminiscing. We also sing when a song belongs to the particular kind of reminiscing we are doing. Most taxi drivers I have met were once GI's. The conversation starts like this: "Last time I saw you. . ." *See* AMERICAN SOLDIER

TEA

The British have an umbilical cord which has never been cut and through which tea flows constantly. It is curious to watch them in times of sudden horror, tragedy or disaster. The pulse stops apparently, and nothing can be done, and not one move made, until a "nice cup of tea" is quickly made. There is no question that it brings solace and does steady the mind. What a pity all countries are not so tea-conscious. World-peace conferences would run more smoothly if a "nice cup of tea," or indeed, a samovar, were available at the proper time.

TEACHER

A woman should not set herself up to be her husband's teacher. He is glad he's out of school. He isn't out of it altogether. Whatever the job he holds, there is always some superior who gives orders. The wife has a fine time in that respect. She is the queen of her house. Although she has certain duties to perform, she doesn't lose her job if she neglects them, and when she does fulfill them, it is still for her to choose *when* to make the bed or scrub the kitchen floor. *See* HOUSEWORK

TEASE

Don't.

TEASING

Teach your teen-age daughters *not* to tease boys into physical desire. You might save their lives.

See LOVERS' LANE

TELEPHONE

The "do-it-yourself" craze invaded telephony. But the customer has to do the work *without* getting a reward for his efforts. The telephone companies do not reduce the rates. They make you work and claim they give you "progressive convenience" long distance dialing. With cunning you can actually materialize a living voice responding to your dialing finger. But no sooner have you sighed forth the name, the number and the town you want to contact, than the ghostly voice intones: Do it youself! Instruction is not included in the kits. You have to *ask* how to proceed, spell town, spell state, spell out where it is near, give lessons in geography. The "just a moment" is the only reminder that you are not talking with a mechanical device.

After the first half hour of your waiting you think fleetingly of hanging up the receiver, but horror strikes you instantly because you know, only too well, that you might never raise the ghost again. You wait and dream. You dream of times when you could give name, town, in cable style to a polite ear on the other end and hear: We'll call you when we have the party on the line.

Suddenly a bad-humoured specter enters your reverie, rattling off numbers that *you must* dial.

And you dial them, good progressive sport that you are. A sudden outburst of all oceans surging into a storm knocks the receiver off you ear. Then silence, then a crackle, then a sweet melody played on a xylophone and then—no ring.

You think: patience, patience, patience. Then you realize that you are holding the dead end of a long dead line. You hang up. You look at the clock. You've spent three quarters of an hour. You are nowhere. You try again. The sound you hear you do not analyze. It may be living, it may be dead; it doesn't matter. The voice says: You can dial that number yourself. You say: I've tried. I got the oceans, the crackles, the music, the silence—but never a ring. The voice says: Dial it again. Are you sure you dialed the correct number??? (That rise in the voice means nothing. The recorded voices do that too.) It's a record, you think. I am pleading with a record. You say: Please help me get the number. The answer: We are not supposed to dial. Do it yourself.

You carry on. You dial this, you dial that. The sounds that greet you vary. But all have this in common: They carry no resemblance to a ring. Your daring finger dials the spectre's number. You tell your story. Urgency speeds your words. The answer, staccato, impersonal: Talk to your special operator. I cannot dial the special operator for you. Do it yourself. . . .

See WESTERN UNION

156

TELEVISION

You can feed your baby peacefully when it's cartoon-time. The toddlers will sit transfixed and still—no mischief will be done, no cries of falls will jar your heart. In the "good old days" an aunt would come, read stories so you could do your chores. But aunts now live in other towns, it seems. You know how long your peace will last, the programs are a clock sounding the hours.

Then there are hours for the older children which bring enjoyment. And there are hours when they learn by sound *and* image what they would *never* learn from books they read in haste and, hastily, forget.

Then there are programs which outspeed the papers in bringing news to you, and they cause you to wonder how long ago it was you trekked to newsreel theatres. And that you loved the "March of Time."

There is the man the country chose, and you can see him near and read his eyes.

There are foreign leaders, the countries, the debates, and you have never left your home.

And then there are the programs for which you never would have left your home (dragging along the youngsters)—now poised and ready to invade your home, materialized by one turn of the knob.

The violence, debauchery, the sugar-dripping falsity, glorified depravity, vulgarity—the age-old reagents of allurement are there to *search you out.*

Don't turn the knob.

. . .And then there are the westerns.

TENDERNESS

Tenderness is greater proof of love than the most passionate of vows.   *See* CON AMORE

157

TERRA FIRMA

Only when one has felt an earthquake seesawing underneath one's feet can one appreciate terra firma.

TEST

Doubt's parasite.

THOMAS, DANNY

My friend. My teacher in the art of making people laugh, people who not only don't want to laugh, but who would prefer not being there watching you. He can drum better on two dirty helmets than many can on the best pair of bongo drums.

TIES

If those multicoloured horrors make you feel carefree and gay, wear them. If they don't have that effect on you, wear them only if your mother has given them to you at Christmas, birthdays or Father's Day. Be sure to wear one when you visit her on Mother's Day. Your wife should be instructed to let you choose your own ties.

See MEN'S CLOTHES

TILLY, VESTA

It has often been written that I was the first performer to wear top hat and tails on the stage. Vesta Tilly and Ella Shields did it first years and years before me.

TIMES

I can truthfully say that times were always bad as long as I can remember.

TIMING

The alpha and omega of aerialists, jugglers, actors, diplomats, publicists, generals, prizefighters, revolutionists, financiers, dictators, lovers.

TODD, MICHAEL

Second-rate people disliked him. That was fine with him and me.

TOLERANCE

Teach it to your children. It is most important to the saving of their souls.

TOMATOES

For cooking, stewing, for all salads, or even if you serve plain sliced tomatoes, take off the skin. Pour boiling water over the tomatoes you have put into a bowl. In a few seconds take them out of the water, the skin comes off easily. If you are in a hurry, hold each one poked on a fork over the open flame for a few seconds. The skin comes off almost as easily.

TRADITION

A treasure and a burden.

TRANSLATION

Goethe gave it the ax. He said: "Translation arouses an irresistible longing for the original."

TRAVEL

To lose your prejudices you must travel.

TRAVELLERS

Don't detain travellers.   *See* LOVE, 3

TRUE LOVE

It's a flower: *Trillium erectum.* Also called birthroot and bethflower. Medicinal use: astringent.

TUBEROSES

The only time I sleep with closed windows is when I have tuberoses in the room. I jealously keep the smell all for myself. They taste good too.

TUNA

Here is another one of those quick, emergency dinners. Open a can of tuna fish. Pour the oil from the can into a frying pan. Add some olive oil—or corn oil. Cut a shallot very fine. Cut a skinned tomato very fine, leaving out the seeds. Braise all in the oil. When tender add the tuna from the can. Turn gently with a wooden spoon. Salt. Pepper. A bit of cream. If you want. Make a couple of slices of toast. Put them on a plate and pour the contents of the pan onto them. A glass of white wine with this. Beer is good too.

TURNIPS

I was raised almost entirely on turnips and potatoes, but I think that the turnips have more to do with the effect than the potatoes.   *See* POTATOES

TWILIGHT

An important time of the day, forever lost to us in cities. Sitting on a bench in front of a house in the country, in the mountains, in villages. . . .Seeing twilight fall should be prescribed by doctors. *See* PEACE

TYNAN, KENNETH

Food for my brain and always on the table when I needed it.

The Blonde Venus, 1932. Cary Grant, Marlene Dietrich.

U GLY DUCKLING

Lucky is the ugly duckling. Keep that in mind and don't
envy the pretty duckling. The dizzy pursuit of pleasure
the pretty duckling easily succumbs to, does not tempt
you constantly. You have time to think, to be alone, to
be lonely, to read, to make friends, to help other people.
You'll be a *happy* swan. Just wait and see.

See BEAUTY *(The Seamy Side)*

ULCER

In bygone days, when the doctor told a patient that he
had an ulcer, the patient was alarmed looking at the list
of forbidden foods, but didn't doubt the cure. Today he
looks alarmed at his spouse, his friends, his boss, his
unfulfilled hopes and wishes, and again at his spouse,
and the cure seems impossible.

ULTIMATUM

I can't stand ultimatums, particularly not in connection with emotional decisions. The person giving an ultimatum is necessarily the stronger one and is taking advantage of this position.

UNIFORM

Makes poor and rich look alike.   *See* ARMY

UNION

L'union fait la force. Union makes strength. To reunite what was divided by the conqueror is a dangerous undertaking for the erstwhile conqueror.

UNITED KINGDOM

I have a sane and quiet love for the country, for the people, the climate, the skies of England; even the fog does not disturb me. I rather like it in the early morning when you have electric light with your tea. I have worked in England and felt at home there. I love the English sense of humour, the tradition-bound habits, the shop-keepers and the pubs. When you see English children you wish you could migrate there with yours.

UNMADE BED

A man would prefer to come home to an unmade bed and a happy woman than to a neatly made bed and an angry woman.

UP

Look there.

USEFULNESS

"Count the day lost whose low descending sun
Views from thy hand no worthy action done."

Anon.

See IDLENESS

UTMOST

When people say, "I'm doing my utmost," they are underestimating themselves greatly.

UXORIOUS

Don't be that, whatever you do, don't become that. You have a better chance to keep your wife by beating her.

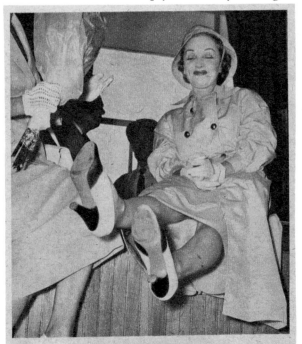

STADIG VERDENS KØNNESTE

Stadig verdens kønneste, ikke sandt? lo den ungdommelige bedstemor Marlene Dietrich (52), da hun kom flyvende fra Paris til Rom og viste sine nysselige og højt forsikrede pusselanker i en ny interessant vinkel. Marlene Dietrich er kommet til Italien for at være med i indspilningen af filmen »The Monte Carlo Story«, hvor hendes partnere bliver Vittorio de Sica og Mischa Auer. Den evigunge Marlene debuterede 1928 i filmen »Kvinden man længes efter«, men slog først afgørende igennem to aar senere i »Den Blaa Engel«.

V

ACILLATION

A woman's beauty of heart and mind renders man's vac-
illating emotions constant. Her looks attract him, they
do not keep him.

VANITY

There is a word that should be stricken from Love's
vocabulary. And from woman's heart and soul and mind.
How many irreparable errors are being made because of
vanity. How weak the voice of love becomes—true and
unfailing though it is—next to the peacock cry of vanity.

And hand in hand with vanity goes pride when it is
used to influence decisions of the heart. How many men
and women parted, how many of them let it happen,
that fatal, final parting, because the woman was too
proud to beg and plead and speak her love. A woman
in moments of distress and injured feelings calls on her

pride to help her take a stand. A stand she thinks she must uphold. Therefore, she says what she has heard and learned of pride, and pride throws words at him and makes him go.

Pride doesn't last once it has done the harm; the heart cries louder with the passing hours and if the tears could bring him back just then, there would be no more pride to bar his way. But it is rare that he comes back just then, when the true values and true feelings lie there open. All too often he arrives when friends have talked, advice was given and pride was once more called upon to turn events in the matters of the heart.

The woman, though, when all is said and done, stands there alone, her lover gone, her love without an aim. Her pride is satisfied, but that won't dry her tears.

See PRIDE

VARIETY

Variety is the spice of life only when it is not for its own sake.

VEAL KIDNEYS

Another one of those dishes to be made while your man or your guests are sitting at the table. You prepare it ahead of time, but that also takes only a few minutes.

Take the skin off the kidneys. You need four or six for two. Cut, with a very sharp knife, very thin slices of the kidney around the hard center of the kidney. Do not cut through the muscles. You waste a bit that way, but it is worth it. Just cut around the main muscle until there is no more meat to cut. Leave the slices on the board. Cover them with foil or a thin kitchen towel.

Heat butter golden brown in a medium-sized frying pan. Add one laurel leaf from the beginning. When the butter is very hot, just before turning brown, throw the sliced kidneys into it. Salt, pepper. Mix fast. Take out laurel leaf. See to it that all slices touch the bottom of the pan repeatedly. In one or two minutes the slices are done. Quickly sprinkle a tiny bit of flour through a fine sieve onto them, turn, and when flour has thickened a bit add a tablespoonful of dry white wine. Mix quickly and onto the platter or individual plates. This is what the French call *La Grande Cuisine* because it all depends on your speed and your ability to guess what cannot be foretold in seconds and minutes.

You serve rice with it and lettuce or romaine, but stay away from strong dressings. The taste of the kidneys is very delicate. Don't spoil it. Drink white wine with this, naturally.

VEGETATE

Lots of people do.

VENUS

Until they come to see us from their planet, I wait patiently. I hear them saying: Don't call us, we'll call you.

VICES

What other people have.

VICTOIRE DE SAMOTHRACE

At the Musée du Louvre they put all the Greek ladies together, their cool breasts casting shadows on the blinding whiteness of their bodies. The most exquisite of

Venuses, Aphrodites, Dianas, stand, stone on stone, weird in their stillness and their rivalry.

You lift your eyes from their rounded shoulders and high upon what seems a hundred stairs stands—no—*walks* "La Victoire de Samothrace." Wind flattens cloth against her ribs, her thighs; you see the strength of widely rooted wings. There is more beauty in her than in all the ladies below. I think it is because besides her beauty, she is doing something. The other ladies are idle.

VICTORY

Victory is gay only back home. Up front it is joyless.

VIENNA

Most nations think that the Viennese used to dance in the streets day and night. They never did.

VILLAGE

The place to live in peace.   *See* TWILIGHT

VIOLETS

I like the wild ones and the garden violets that smell strongly. The hothouse ones one can just as well leave in the hothouse.

VIOLIN

The symbol of my broken dream.

VIRTUE

You have to make your own laws and rules about that; not much you have learned in theory quite fits the praxis.

Losing your virtue might be considered virtuous by the fellow you lost your virtue to. But in the eyes of the other fellow, who wasn't that lucky, or of your father and mother, you are a low and "fallen woman" by one and the same deed. If the man you lost your virtue to marries you, you are just lucky—not more virtuous than the next girl who didn't catch the guy. And later, you are a madonnalike creature to the man you leave your husband for, and again, by the same deed, you are a "rotten-to-the-core" adulteress to your husband, his kin and the neighbors. Just by these few examples, you can see how mixed up a girl can get about the meaning of virtue. So you must make, and live by, your own code of virtue. It is rewarding, as the saying goes, whereas deserting one's own code brings disastrous consequences.

VISCONTI, LUCHINO

It was easy for him to enthrall, enlight, dominate, instruct, bewitch all without even trying.

VITAMINS

They used to come in the food. They don't come in the food anymore. You have to take them. Pills, capsules, drops.   *See* RICKETS

VODKA

I spent a large part of my early youth with Russian people. I first learned how to cook Russian dishes and when I was older I learned how to drink vodka. It is one of the more healthy drinks in the alcohol field. When the Third Army had made contact with the Russians

during the Second World War we drank a lot of it. The
Russian troops which we entertained had an unending
supply. *See* CHOCOLATE

VOICE

If beautiful voices were sold over the counter prettily
wrapped, women would buy them. Too bad they aren't.

MARLENE DIETRICH
The daughter of an army officer killed before World War I, Marlene launched her film career in Germany in 1923, became an international star in '29 with **The Blue Angel.** Brought to America by Josef von Sternberg in 1930, she started the vogue for women's slacks. By the time she made **Destry Rides Again,** in '39, she was an American citizen and an American legend. In '53, she became a singing star in night clubs. Last year she was the first woman to receive Israel's Medallion of Honor . . . just another of the world's many tributes to her.

AR

If you haven't been in it, don't talk about it.

WASTE

I hate it with a passion.   *See* ENGLISH

WEAKNESS

The weak are more likely to make the strong weak than the strong are likely to make the weak strong.

WEALTH

The power wealth gives is a dangerous power, especially in the hands of the wealthy.

WEIN CHAUD D'EAU

Four yolks of eggs, seven flat spoons of sugar mixed in a bowl till creamy. The more creamy the better the chaud d'eau. Add a cup of dry white wine and stir.

171

Transfer into double boiler. Beat with eggbeater (by hand) till mixture rises, is warm and has the consistency of thick foam. Don't let it boil over but keep beating till the foam just drips off your eggbeater when you lift it out. You need a large double boiler, because the mixture rises to almost double its amount. If you are a good cook you do it on the open low flame as then you can use any pot that is not too wide, but high. Serves four including seconds.

WEISS BEER

Made for the very thirsty. A pale summer beer. Drink it in a large, wide open glass. You can buy it in stores that carry German imports.

WELLES, ORSON

When I have seen him and talked with him, I feel like a plant that has been watered. His brilliant mind is coupled with a simple and practical heart. He is generous with both.

WELTSCHMERZ

The pain, the sorrow of the world that at moments grips the heart of the individual.

WEST, MAE

A milestone, a catchword, sex with its tongue in its cheeks.

WESTERN UNION

When you call Western Union on the telephone you get a busy signal. Should you *not* get a busy signal, hang up. You have dialed a wrong number. But should you finally be lucky enough to slip in between the thousand calls, you *do* hear the living voice of a living operator. This operator

1) sounds businesslike, but with a friendly overtone;
2) does not accentuate the words as if you were an idiot who can't answer a straight question;
3) suggests ways of sending wires or cables;
4) behaves all round good "like" an operator should.

When I try to make contact with Western Union and the busy signal lullabies my ear, I send an urgent prayer to Hermes; to keep this earthly branch un-progressively in status quo—lullaby and all—and to keep on the other end of the line the living responses, the living efficiency, the living inefficiency, the goodwill and sympathy the human brain excels in.　　　*See* TELEPHONE

WESTERN WORLD

"It is closing time in the gardens of the Western world."

Cyril Connolly

WHITE BREAD

I cringe every time I see a child eating a sandwich made out of American white bread. Give them whole wheat or rye bread if you love your children.

WHITNEY, BETSEY CUSHING

A beautiful woman. I met her many years ago and she impressed me deeply. I saw her very rarely—at a crowded party, at a theatre while people were pushing by, or from faraway we waved to each other. She was warm and kind, tolerant, reserved and shy and had the wisdom of a child. She was a mother, and I think the day I saw her with her children I knew why she was attractive to me. You know more about a woman when you see her with her children than she or anybody else can tell you. A real mother doesn't change her attitude toward her children when strangers are around. That was the first thing I noticed. The children did not have the puzzled look you see so often, when Mother isn't Mother anymore but some strange lady, strangely gay and loving or strangely stern, coaxing with a smile that isn't hers. I still remember her that day; she sat quietly, the children talked, the sun shone through the windows and singled her out.

WHITSUNTIDE

My favorite holiday, beginning with Whitsunday, the seventh Sunday after Easter. In many European countries green branches, mostly from birch trees, are put in front of houses in water buckets and the children wear white.

WIDOW

A good custom in some European countries: A widow wears both her own and her husband's wedding ring on her finger.

WIFE

Any wife will come through with flying colours in an emergency or when facing a dramatic challenge. To come through with flying colours when married life runs on routine tracks marks the *truly* good wife.

WILDER, BILLY

A master builder who knows his tools and uses them expertly to frame out the structure on which he hangs the garlands of his wit and wisdom.

WILL

It is almost impossible to put on paper what one would want done after one is dead.

WIND

When you stand in the wind you are acutely aware of being alive. This is a place as good as any to write down the words of George Borrow which move me deeply:

"There's night and day, brother, both sweet things; sun, moon, and stars, brother, all sweet things; there's likewise a wind on the heath. Life is very sweet, brother; who would wish to die?"

WINES

Of all the wines I have drunk, I like best the *gros vin rouge,* the ordinary wine the French drink instead of water. It is issued on ration cards when times are hard and members of the army and navy receive their daily ration in peace as well as war.

WISDOM

"For in much wisdom is much grief: and he that increaseth knowledge increaseth sorrow." *Ecclesiastes 1:18*
See GRIEF

WISHES

The wishes of a mother for her child are few; they can be held in a baby's hand.

WITHHOLDING TAX

The United States Government's hijacking of the wage-earner's private property, depriving him of the use of such property during the tax year and benefiting the banking concerns of the country. *See* ESTIMATED TAX

WOMEN

"If all the harm that women have done
Were put in a bundle and rolled into one,
　　　Earth would not hold it,
　　　The sky could not enfold it,
It could not be lighted nor warmed by the sun."

James Kenneth Stephen

They didn't "mean to," Mr. Stephen.

WORDS, 1

Words can bruise and break hearts, and minds as well. There are no black and blue marks, no broken bones to put in plaster casts, and therefore no prison bars for the offender.

WORDS, 2

Lover's words: "How beautiful you are, now that you love me."

WORDS, 3

Once lovers have exhausted the simple talk of lovers, describing the glory of it all, and have agreed on the words and feelings on their first meeting, they should stop talking. It is inevitable that words straying outside of this narrow circle will bring disharmony.

WORRY

Dr. Charles Mayo said that worry affects the circulation, the heart, the glands, the nervous system. I wish he would give constructive thought to a remedy. Not for the ordinary worries each human carries in his heart, but for the harder worries borne of a hurried doctor's honest verdict.

WRITING

The laws of the written style are to me the same as of the spoken style. The tempo of a sentence is so important to me that only when the tempo is just right does the meaning seem clear.

X

ANTHIPPE

If the wife of Socrates was the prototype of a quarrelsome woman, it is quite natural that the man of normal wisdom cannot cope with his own Xanthippe. I wonder how long Socrates would have stood it.

See QUARREL

XMAS

An abbreviation which should be forbidden by the police.

See CHRISTMAS

X RAY

In American slang: a ten thousand dollar bill.

See SLANG

Y

ARDSTICK

I have "yardstick" eyes. It is very convenient. I can also tell if a given pitcher or pot will hold a given amount of liquid or solid. This is particularly convenient in the kitchen.

YEAST

I go to a lot of trouble to get fresh yeast. I wheedle it out of French bakeries most of the time.

I cannot stand (or measure) dehydrated yeast; it doesn't smell or behave like real yeast.

YELLOW

The gayest of all colours. Yellow walls make a sunny room.

YOGURT

When a baby pulls up his knees and fusses or cries he usually has air in his lower stomach. Ask your pediatrician what he thinks of a tiny bit of yogurt to ease his pains and your nerves. *See* BABY CARE

YOUTH

Youth is optimism and trust.

Die Frau nach der man sich sehnt, with Fritz Kortner

Film star Marlene Dietrich lightened up the heart of many a lonely GI in World War II. USO entertainers were also of tremendous help in the Korean conflict.

ABAGLIONE

Mix three yolks of eggs with three tablespoons of sugar until the mixture is creamy and whitish. Then add a bit more than half a cup of Marsala wine. Mix. In a double boiler beat the mixture with an eggbeater till it rises. Do not boil the mixture. Use a large enough pot so that it can rise almost to double the amount. If you are courageous you can forget about the double boiler and do it on a direct low flame.

Serve it in wide-top glasses while it is warm.

See WEIN CHAUD D'EAU

ZEITGEIST

Germans are accused, and rightfully so, of needing a lot of words where the English need one. Here is an exception. *Zeitgeist* means the spirit of the age, the feeling of a period.

ZEPHYR

I like the wind, the wool, the soft cloth they make in Belgium.

ZEPPELIN

My first inkling that all was not "fair in war" came to me at a very early age.

My uncle Max Dietrich was captain of the Zeppelin which was to drop a bomb on Manchester during World War I. When the German Kaiser learned that his cousin the King of England happened to be in Manchester on that certain day he ordered the Zeppelin to return with the mission uncompleted. The Zeppelin was shot down over the ocean by the British. My aunt never believed that my uncle was dead and waited for his return long after the war ended.

ZIPPER

The frustration caused by a stuck zipper is indescribable. Learn to repair zippers. You will save time, nerves, money.

ZITHER

Nostalgic sound with memories of mountains and meadows and summer in Austria.

ZWIEBACK

Symbol of childhood days.

Good to have around the house. Makes a quick dessert for children. Soak three broken-up zwieback in a small bowl or cup in cold or warm milk, press down with a spoon, add honey to taste. When you turn it over onto a plate, it should keep the form. Sprinkle with sugar if you have no honey. Children love to prepare this themselves.

/e

.?

writing. When Shan[
gan, drowning in h[
sive wish to convinc[
that he is a black[
genius of a jazz [
fails pitifully, the[
falters because we [
expecting it for [
Even an exceptio[
cise performance [

Black
John-
r fig-
Black

Thompson as Shan[
bring the scene of[
cide of Dee, John[
hooker (played in a[
ic opera style [
Pearson) is also c[
up for us and[
ruined.

lened
guish
)rand
But
per-
) all
here
e us
nally
con-
een,
and
the
1 or
hese
t, in
de-

Elsewhere, and [
ten, the play's nur[
matic values go [
explored. Several [
ers speak in a fas[
all but incom[
Transitions are sl[
dled, one scene c[
the next, the di[
eptness leading [
"move" the play[
tactics as having[
open and slam [
der to guide ev[
mood toward en[
exits. Beyond th[
Cornell's notion [
or holding tensio[
actors talk right [
cal pauses; all o[
failing him, he [
stage lights.

(—
1 at
the
be-
abe
ully
:hat
ba-
atic
has
are
nes
ack
ine
ose
)n-
ex-
gi-

True, the play[
That doesn't h[
Some of the ch[
teresting though[
long in Gordone [
(Let us pray ther[
Moreover, Go[
trol of his wo[
ally lapses, t[
play into som[
areas. At such [

lic
)m

nous rumble is [
picion of self-h[
hint of contem...

M/
he

his picture the year before
of Eisenstaedt" (Viking).

In 1954 in liberation of Paris ceremony